MW01292574

FOREWORD

I'M *still* OLD FASHIONED!

REAL.RAW.UNCUT.

Markita D. COLLINS

All Rights Reserved. No part of this publication may be reproduced in any form or by any means, including scanning, photocopying, or otherwise without prior written permission of the copyright holder. This book is licensed for your personal enjoyment only. It must not be re-sold but can be purchased and given away to other people. If you would like to share this book with another person, please purchase an additional copy for each person at: AMAZON.COM or places where my books are sold. If you are reading this book and did not purchase it, or it was not purchased for your use only, then please go to the online bookstore and purchase your own copy.

Disclaimer and Terms of Use: The Author and Publisher has tried to be as accurate and complete as possible in the creation of this book, notwithstanding the fact that she does not warrant or represent at any time that the contents within are accurate due to the rapidly changing nature of the internet. While all attempts have been made to verify information provided in this publication the Author and Publisher assumes no responsibility for errors, omissions, or contrary interpretation of the subject matter therein. Any perceived slights of specific persons, peoples, or organizations are unintentional. In practical advice books, like anything else in life, there are no guarantees. This book is not intended for use as a source for legal, business, accounting or financial advice. All readers are advised to seek the services of competent professionals in the legal, business, accounting and finance field.

Cover Design by: Ali LaShaun Collins –
www.Uimaginemedia.com
Publisher: The Princess of Suburbia® Publishing –
http://bit.ly/millionaireinfluencersecrets
http://www.drfumihancock.com
Author: Markita D. Collins - Imagine Media, LLC.
www.MarkitaDCollins.com

[handwritten inscription: Taj, My dear! all is well! I'm Still watching 2018]

I'm *Still* OLD FASHIONED!

REAL.RAW.UNKUT.

GLOBAL EDITION

MARKITA D. COLLINS
Bestselling Author

FOREWORD BY REAL TALK KIM

Copyright © 2018 Markita D. Collins
ISBN 10:1721776087
ISBN 13: 978-1721776085
All rights reserved.

DEDICATION

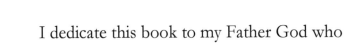

I dedicate this book to my Father God who
is in Heaven and continues to live in my heart.
Thank you, Abba!
I dedicate this book to my Lord and savior Jesus
Christ! You died and rose with all power just for me.
It's through you that I live and have my being.

I dedicate this book to my husband Ali
"Shaun" Collins. You are the reason why "I'm
still a little old fashioned." That's right baby!

I dedicate this book to my Daddy and
Mommy, Richard and Linda Faye. God really
loves me, he gave me the best parents this

side of heaven. You get to enjoy the fruit of
your labor.

I dedicate this book to all the women and
men that have been and will be blessed by my
journey and personal growth and
transformation.

.

CONTENTS

MARKITA D. COLLINS

ACKNOWLEDGMENTS

There are so many people I would like to acknowledge at this time. However, I would be writing forever.

To my ministry friends and family from all over the world, I love you all, and I'm honored you would see me as a sister and friend.

Thank you to every person that has sown into my life and has been a blessing to me and my family.

Thank you to every WIFE I've learned from, watched and gleaned from my whole life! To every WIFE who wants to do it "The Old-Fashioned Way" and not lose who you are. I am praying for you. I pray this book ministers, encourages and inspires you.

Thank you to Prophet Marcus and Lady Sharita Rivers for being our friends and covering us during a time of great transition.

Thank you to Apostle Louis Dickens, you just came in and made things very plain. We love you! I know this book wouldn't have happened if these two men of God that I mentioned didn't speak over me at such a hard and crucial time. Pastor Albert Walker "Grandpa" (Rest well, everything you said is happening we won't let you down) and Pastor Tony Kemp. I obeyed the Lord, and yes, I finally wrote! Love you so much.

To my amazing Markita D. Collins Team…still Shaun and Robyn! (lol) It's funny but so true that we are great together! Robyn…sis your part in my life was so timely. And for that I am grateful. Thank you for everything.

To Kim Poither aka Real Talk Kim! I asked, and your answer was yes! No questions asked. You've always been so kind and supportive to me since I met you. Kim, I appreciate, and love you.

Dr. Princess Fumi Hancock! I'm still trying to figure out how and why? But I will say thank you for your obedience to GOD and making sure that I didn't drop this baby. This was not a mistake! It's working for our Good! You really are a midwife!

To my amazing supporters of *Girl Talk with Kita* and *Kita's Kompany* – I love y'all. You all blow me away! Thanks for loving me and supporting everything I do. As your leader, advisor, coach and instructor, I thank you from the bottom of my heart!

To the wonderful young people that call me "Auntie," TT, God mom and Mom. You are a radical bunch and you ROCK! I stay "LIT" because of y'all! Thank you for trusting me with your hearts. Thank you for fighting for me and believing in me all the way. You matter to me. I am so proud to know you.

Daddy and Mommy, I am full of tears right now because I know you can read this part repeatedly.

Over 40 years of marriage. THAT'S A MIRACLE. Daddy you have protected, provided, loved, fought for, and worked countless hours for your "girls." It's not often nowadays that fathers are even around to raise their children in one home to one wife. Thank you, daddy, for being my number 1 guy! You were the first man to ever love me! You taught me how to love people past their faults. You showed me how to be true to who I am…and to never let one monkey stop the show. You showed me that people will be people, and that doesn't change who we are. I love you for showing up for me time and time again. You were there during the worst times and greatest times. You never made me feel like I was too far not to come back home. I'll always be your "boogie" & Keet! Forever!

Mommy, Mommy, Mommy…you birthed me; you loved me; you spanked my butt and didn't play games with me! You felt every pain I ever endured. You taught me how to be a lady and never lose my self-worth. I remember an event which occurred and you said to me "No, not my child, if he doesn't want you let him go! You have Kent blood in you!" (tears) Mommy while you fought forces and were ridiculed, you found the strength to cover me in OIL and prayer! You required that I be a strong woman, but to always honor my father and husband. Thank you so much Mommy for being the rock you are to me!

To my Aunt Hattie and my Godfather Joe who is gone to be with the Lord...though you're not here, you were in my heart the whole time during this journey.

To my little sisters LaTrisha and Tracy: there are no words to describe the bond which we share. I love you! To my brothers in-law Garrett, Darreese and my nieces and nephew, I love you too! We are truly an amazing family! No matter what we face we always come together. We laugh; we fight; we pray; we forgive; we love; we honor; and we protect and cherish one another. That's what FAMILY does! Nothing can keep us apart.

Clarence the only thing that makes us not related

is DNA! Thank you for being the greatest brother ever. We grew up in the same play pin and still closer than ever!

I want to acknowledge my whole entire family (Birdens, Kents, Cummingses, Littletons, Skipps, Collinses), Aunties, Uncles, Godmothers, Papas, sisters, brothers, cousins, all of you, both natural and spiritual.

Special love goes to all my godchildren – all 7 of you!

I want to thank God for the people I've met along the way that have stayed and those who are gone.

Last but not least, I must acknowledge my wonderful husband and beautiful children! Josiah, Moriah, Mikaila, and Destin. Mommy loves you so very much. To my gift Aliana, you taught me how to be a great "Mother." Mimi loves you. One day you will ask me hard questions and I will be here for you to answer them.

Shaun, well here it is babe. I never knew that

things would turn out this way with you and me.
You are the reason it's easy to be a good wife.
You're such an incredible husband. Being married to
you makes me forget about the hurt that I endured
in my past. You really helped me to let my guard
down and stop being so angry. I'll never forget the
day when you grabbed me and said "I'm not them! I
won't hurt you!" That broke something in me and it
never came back. You sir are so appreciated, and my
life has been far better since you found me. I thank
God for you Ali "Shaun". I really do.

I went from being broken to being healed. Now I'm
whole because I've learned life's lessons. GOD is a
good GOD and I will forever be grateful to Him for
this moment right here and now. There's more to
come...Thank you Jesus...There is much more to
come!

~Mrs. Markita D. Collins

MARKITA D. COLLINS

FOREWORD

"I'm still old fashioned" is such a great reminder that we as women are life givers. We as women can make or break our worlds with what we carry on the inside of us. We can make a poor man feel righteous. That is why the enemy fights us so hard in our emotions. He knows one woman can change the trajectory of her whole family. When a woman is healed and walking in her God ordained purpose as a woman, she is a game changer.

When God created Adam He created Adam because He wanted to, but when He created Eve, He created her because He had to. Women bring forth life. Society will have us believing that we have to look a certain way, have so many degrees, act a certain way in order to be accepted. But, not with God on our side. All we have to be is whole. Confident in who God created us to be. Walking on purpose and in purpose.

This book that Markita wrote will equip you and get you focused on being a woman of graceful power. She is revealing so much truth and life in these pages.

Some things my friend mentions may even surprise you however her story and the wisdom God has placed in Markita's life speaks with POWER and TRUTH.

The fact is A STRONG Woman wears the look of confidence on her face, but a woman of STRENGTH wears a Couture Fashion called "GRACE."

I'M STILL OLD FASHIONED!

A CALLED WOMAN finds no need to compete with other women. She recognizes there is only ONE of her, and authenticity stands alone.

Kimberly Jones Pothier, Founder & CEO, Conquering Hell in High Heels
https://realtalkkim.com/

MARKITA D. COLLINS

ENDORSEMENT

"Markita Collins continues to raise the bar as it to entrepreneurship and that bar has been raised even further with the release of her latest book, "A Little Old Fashioned Goes A Long Way." It pertains is an easy read with fundamental principles that today's society is indeed lacking."

-Hasan James, Editor-In-Chief, Root Magazine

"This book was so good I literally read it in 2 sittings. It grabs you in the beginning, convicts you and helps you in the end. Markita's transparency & transformation are inspiring so you feel like you have

a friend in life's struggles as you read it! I'd suggest this for single, married, divorced, just everyone cause you will find a piece of yourself within these pages!"
-*Liris Crosse, Super Model*

"Tangibility, transparency and ownership are lacking in today's social media driven ethos. Markita D. Collins stands out as a forward thinking woman of God, who is not cloaked or steeped in religious dogma. With her healing and transparent book, A Little Old Fashioned Goes a Long Way, Markita gives readers a brutally honest view of her life. Moreover, she provides the tender love and care to see to it that her audience learns from her mistakes and thrive in life. Authenticity is a rare commodity today. Markita D. Collins and A Little Old Fashioned Goes a Long Way are steeped in its richness. The book is pure gold. Be Great!!"
-*Pervis Taylor, III, M.A*

PREFA CE

One thing people can never say about me is that I am not honest with them and real. I may not be perfect nor claim to be perfect. I do know that "I'm still old fashioned RAW and UNCUT" story needed to be told. Why? I'll tell you… because I am in a different space than before. There were stories and truths I wanted to share in my first edition, that I couldn't.

To my old followers, hold on to your seats because the things I am revealing you never heard from me before. To all the new people reading this, the journey is real so get ready. No doubt about it, new chapters and nuggets of wisdom have been added to my life. I feel that I owe it to you the reader to be open and transparent. With confidence, I am anointed to speak to the single woman, the married woman and the divorced woman. It matters not where you are in life or what your circumstances are. My message is not one for the faint at heart or for those that want to make excuses, I couldn't make excuses. I wonder where I would be now, if I did.

There is not a relationship situation that I have not been part of. That's right. I can speak to it because I've been through it. And it took all of that for me to be able to say this. I am not a "girlfriend". I am not a "wifey". I am not a "Booh". I am not a "Bae". I am a wife! I am not a push over! I am not a door mat! I am not just some random "chick". I am a Lady, a woman, a wife, mother, leader, mentor and friend!

You see with this book, I came to embrace the real lady and woman in me. I like what I have become. The truth is I wasn't so sure if I really had what it took to succeed. Well not only did I succeed but overcame!

Maybe where you are right now is that you are single, and you want to be married. Or if you're married, you want it to be better. Or divorced and just need some encouragement. You need to know that your blessing is not going to always come through familiar avenues. It's not going to come through what is known and comfortable to you. Sometimes it's going to come through ways that are unexpected. God's going to do it that way so that you know it's Him, and you won't be able to doubt it if you tried. Stop trying to make it come the way you want it to. Stop trying to force it or speed it up. This thing has to marinate in you. It has to settle in your heart, in your spirit. It has to take its time to get to you without you mucking up the works. You've got to surrender in this process and you've got to wait on it, not beg but wait. Wait. Wait without struggle. Wait without complaining. Wait without anger and frustration. Wait and know you're going to reap because girlfriend, you're not going to faint!

As a matter of fact guess what? According to Ezra 10:4 those assigned to you will come. You will have to rise up and know that the matter is in your hands and you got this! It may not come from people who know your "right now" story or those from your past. I have come to realize that they cannot hold the vision and the intention for your next story. Be careful who you share this journey with. Be sure they can handle what's on the inside of you. My dear, your job is to be in the receptive position to obtain the gift of blessing. Then as the blessing grows within you, you must move to the birthing position to see it manifest. Your blessing is coming from a divine place of love and purpose. You will not miss it if you stay the course. You will not sabotage it if you stay the course. You will surely see the Glory of the Lord for you in this if you do not get weary.

"I'm still old fashioned" is going to take you on a greater pathway.

Watch out now! Enjoy this journey. I did.

INTRODUCTION...KING SAYS

The *king* says...

I can recall walking into my 10th grade Biology class; it was day three of my first year at a new school. In walks this cute "chocolate girl" with a big smile and an even bigger air of boldness and confidence about her. I couldn't help but to notice how she commanded the attention of everybody in the room, but seemed to handle it with an "effortless grace."

This intrigued me, as I lacked that degree of confidence and boldness: It was in that moment I made up my mind that she would be mine one day. Now, I don't know if it was love back then, but you can definitely say it was desire at first sight.

Somehow I knew that everything I discerned in that first glance, were qualities I wanted and needed next to me (and did I mention she was cute?!).

A few weeks after that, we were in class watching *The Miracle of Life* (which, as you can imagine, was an experience for a classroom full of fifteen-year-olds), and up until this point I had developed a crush on this "chocolate girl," but hadn't mustered up enough courage to even speak to her. So in typical Thunder Kat fashion, she taps me on the shoulder and says, "Hi! I'm Markita. What's your name?" "Shaun," I replied. Her next question set the foundation for the lady I would grow to know and love...she said, "Hi Shaun. That was an interesting movie. So what does it feel like when boys have sex?!" And thus the first Girl Talk was born.

When I think about life with my Wife, I liken it to driving a car. When you drive, you can't always just floor it and to get where you want to be safely; you have to learn exactly when to accelerate and when to pump the brakes. There is a wisdom and a balance to driving, understanding the flow of traffic, while adhering to rules of the road.

The same is true for me as a husband to a strong wife. To arrive at our intended destination, there are times when I have to fall back and allow her to be who she is; there are times when I have to press and remind her of who I am!

Now, are there some "rules of engagement" when it comes to marriage and relationships? Yes. But I've learned to establish our own flow while keeping the "rules" in mind.

This "flow" is only established through communication, and I'm not talking about a one-sided, finger-pointing, victimized, monologue form of communication. I'm talking about a DIALOGUE, Hearing & Listening, Compromise, and Understanding a perspective outside of your own.

The most challenging part about my growth as a husband hasn't been her; it has been learning to humble myself, and letting go of an inherent desire to be the victor in every "battle" of my life.

George Herbert wrote, "Sometimes the best way to gain is to lose." It has been in those moments of "loss" or conceding that I have learned the most about myself and my spouse; those moments of revelation have consistently propelled us to our next level.

I have learned that His strength is made perfect in our weakness; when we embrace our shortcomings and allow God to work through our spouse, we become strong.

A good partner will enhance not hinder; they challenge you to stretch beyond your own expectations, they frustrate "in Love," and when all else fails, they pick up the slack and hold you down until you can get it right.

I have a spouse like this. She has taught me the difference between a woman and a lady; you're born a woman, biology and reproductive organs classify you as such; (most) men are hard wired to

WANT a woman; but a lady, that's what we NEED!

Ladies aren't born, they are developed, through experiences, though trials, through maturation... A Lady personifies class, style, integrity: she knows when it's time to put her earrings on (and Stand), and when it's time to take them OFF (and Fight)!

I've heard it said that a man finds a wife. I would argue that he finds the raw materials for one. God never gives a man a finished product; He gives us the raw materials and charges us to CULTIVATE.

He doesn't give us the leather coat, He hides it in the cow. He doesn't give us a house, He hides the wood in the trees. He doesn't give us the Lady, He hides her in the woman. He doesn't give us the Wife, He hides her in the Lady.

I have been given the tremendous honor of cultivating one of God's greatest gifts; He has allowed me to pour trust, love and wisdom into her from the first day we spoke all those years ago. He has allowed me to be there through heart break, through joy, during the times when she was trying to rediscover who she was. He has allowed me to be there to help shape, mold and cultivate the woman, the lady and the wife I love today.

1.FLASH BACK!

Wait! What is going on?! That can't be what I what I think it is. That was the feeling I had when I saw a beautiful box with a white satin bow around it. The tears and screams I let out when I saw the books that I wrote for the very first time. This moment was one of the greatest experiences of my life. All this hard work and it still felt like a dream. True to form, Shaun was there by my side. To my surprise, he got a little emotional with me too. Finally, we were able to see what we were waiting for… what we had accomplished.

YES! My book was here!

Suddenly the flashes came rushing back. At that moment my mind went back to September 2016. It was time to move again… this time from the south back up north… just a few hours back from our hometown in the state of Pennsylvania. All we had was enough money to move. We did not have the money to do what was to come next… to invest in a book.

When I was approached about writing my own book by a popular entrepreneur and coach, I was startled… I was excited… I was nervous… I was overjoyed and scared… and I was apprehensive. However, after speaking to Shaun and getting some sound advice, we faced the challenge, invested thousands of dollars into this project and it was time to start. Little did we know, at that moment, we were going to face another challenge. It was time to pack up our home and move to Pennsylvania and we had no idea what was ahead, but God knew. We rented portable trailers to move our belongings from Memphis, TN to Southern PA, however, when it was time to pack almost 1/3 of our things didn't fit. The day of pickup and move, we end up having an impromptu yard sale. The kids and I literally flagged cars down! I went on social media to post pictures and told people to hurry down to our place and get these items at crazy low prices. It was just Shaun, the kids and I, like it had always been. We had to get on the road before dark because there was nowhere for us to go, all of our things were en route to PA and we had to turn our keys back in to the owner. So, we fit the rest of what we could in our vehicle and off we went.

On the road again, right around 11pm, we stopped at a hotel to rest. The next day, in the middle of the state of Tennessee, our vehicle broke down on us. It was so hot, at least 95 degrees or more, and I remember being on the highway when it happened. We had pulled off the highway to get on a main road and thank God there was no traffic behind us or coming towards us. Our car went completely dead and remember, it's a hot summer day, the children are hungry, and my husband and I are exhausted! All from driving 7 hours the prior night, stopping at a hotel overnight, and we were nowhere near Pennsylvania.

I'M STILL OLD FASHIONED!

Shaun is frustrated and I'm trying to remain calm and keep the children from being irritated… we just sat in the car for about 5 minutes before realizing what was right in front of us. Keep in mind, this is a time when a lot of racial tension was taking place and many of our men and women were being gunned down by police. We were in front of a police precinct in the middle of Tennessee, but it wasn't your normal police station… it was our miracle place… and I should explain. The first police officer drove by us… he was black, but he didn't stop or even ask us if we were OK, he just kept driving! Then another police officer drove by… he was white and he asked, "Hey, are you folks OK? Do you need any help?" Of course we were nervous, because, again, this was at the height of a lot of racial profiling and shootings, so I looked out the window while on the phone with our friend and I said, "Yes officer". Shaun kept his head down and I said "Our vehicle just broke down." He said, "Let's see if we can get it moved into the parking lot". Shaun tried to start the car and again nothing happened, so the officer helped Shaun push the car into the parking lot. He said, "Folks, it's real hot out here... let's get your kids inside the precinct and let them run around and get cooled off. We have a vending machine in there for some snacks and some sodas." He was just so kind! So we went inside the precinct and Shaun and I were in tears as we felt the kindness and generosity of the officer. I knew we didn't have an extra $500 laying around to rent a car and before we could even say anything, our friends helped us rent a van for the last leg of the trip. The officer called a local tow company and mechanic to check our car and when he arrived he said if we had driven 5 more miles our wheel would've fallen off! It was a miracle we made it half way through TN and this is after we just put $1100 into the car. God is so good! I had to go get the van from the rental place and another officer came to say, "I'll take you to pick up your car, ma'am, no problem". These people were so nice and kind to us, it was mind-blowing.

I went to get the rental and we left our dead vehicle… I knew we would never see it again… and we were off on the road again! Incredible as it may sound… I still can't believe it… on the brand-new minivan the tire blew! We heard a pop and pulled off the highway, got out the van, only to see a flat tire. All I could do was lift my hands and cry out to God. I mean right in the middle of the road, I cried out to GOD. I didn't care who was watching. A big praise came out my mouth. It was getting darker and we are stuck again! People were driving past us and finally four people tried to help… one young lady saying that she would not leave us until help came. I called the closest rental place to get the van replaced and we waited for roadside assistance for over 40 minutes. It was frustrating and now dark and cold. Shaun was trying to figure out where the spare was located on this van.

We got the tire out. Shaun is now exhausted and a big pick-up truck pulls up… it happened to be a Ford F150, and this little, white guy jumps out. He had to be no taller than five feet five and he just looked at my husband and said, "Move out of the way… I got this sir". We looked at him and thought, "What?" He threw that tire on in about 10 minutes! We wanted to bless him with money to say thank you, but he looked at us and said, "I had to do this… your money is no good here". I said, "Well can I pray for you?" He replied, "Yes, please do that and pray for my family". When he looked at the tire that blew there was a gash, as if somebody had stabbed the tire with a knife. We knew it was the grace of God that kept us. We went to the rental place and, guess what? We got the same van but just in a different color! We had to unload and reload again! By this time, we knew we would have to stay another night in TN. So, a trip that was supposed to take 15hrs took two days!

By this time, the devil was talking to me! "All that money you spent for books, seminars and classes… you should get it back and buy a new car! You made a mistake! What are you going to do in a new city with no transportation? You can't borrow any more money from your parents. You are stupid for doing this!" For a quick moment, I felt very heavy in my heart, but then I remembered the vision and shook off that heaviness and began to thank GOD for his provision.

We made it to PA and moved into our new townhome. It was a tough three and half weeks, walking to the store and gas station for food to feed our kids. We got them enrolled in school, thank God, and they rode the bus… we knew they would have breakfast, lunch and a snack. Shaun and I did without for a while, but we trusted the word and voice of the Lord. While working on the book and waiting for everything to come together, we never complained. We never asked for help, we were not on any assistance and God still made sure we all of our needs were still met. Then came the day we had to walk 4 miles in the rain, while the kids were off to school. So, with book bags to fill, Shaun and I went to the grocery store to get food for the house… we had applied for a minivan a few days prior and were just waiting… and waiting. Well, we couldn't keep taking the Uber to get around because they didn't run during the day where we lived and it also became very costly, so most of the time we just walked and walked and walked.

Shaun stopped by a general store and bought me an umbrella, because of the rain, and we held hands and talked all the way to the grocery store. We packed the book bags with our food and back to the house, we started walking. We laughed and started thanking God. I said to Shaun "this will be the last day we walk in the rain like this babe! We are going to have our van!" Well a few blocks from the house, I received a call, "Hello Mrs. Collins? You were approved for your Van! When can you come get it?" Shaun and I were all wet from the rain, but we rejoiced! I called my friend and said, "Sis we got approved! We just have to do one more thing." She said, "I got you! Go get your van!" What?! Shaun and

I hit our knees and cried out to God… "you allowed us to see your hand of provision yet again." We went and the got the van the next day! We didn't ask for help, but God put it on her heart to do so. All while having little to no furniture in the house… just beds, a table, and futon for the kids to use. All this time and the book still wasn't ready for print yet! I was still fired up and motivated! I kept going onto social media, yet no one knew a thing. I got dressed, put my makeup on and showed up with a smile, ministering and encouraging the people daily. I never asked for a dime! I would bake, teach classes, and all while still kept under wraps that I would be launching a book soon. Time stretched… it felt like forever! We just kept holding onto each other, and to

God, like never before. Again, we knew that GOD was going to provide!

Christmas came, and it was a beautiful one! Happy new year, although I suffered greatly in secret with severe back pain, migraines and sciatic nerve pain for 7 months and, yet again, I never complained. February came and went... now it is March 6th, our twin daughters birthday, and to my surprise a package was hand-delivered to us. It was the books we'd been waiting for! Everything changed now.

Shaun embraced me and we broadcast live on my private group, Kita's Kompany, to show them the surprise. The next morning, again, I went live on social media, "Hi! I am Markita D. Collins and I am wife a mother... a woman of faith... entrepreneur and now an author!" I was so excited! I was being interviewed by another best-selling author when it was time to launch the book. Imagine my surprise when, on the first day of my book release, I was able to sell out all of my copies within three hours! Oh my God. You did this!

Everything seemed right. Everything looked right. But something was off. This felt somehow familiar. I had felt this way before. I don't like this feeling at all.

MARKITA D. COLLINS

2. IS THIS TRAIN MOVING?

Were the people going to buy the book? Were they going to enjoy what they read? Did I do a good job? Will it go over well? I had no idea… all I knew is that at that moment, it was GO TIME. And with over 3000 active viewers online, I said, "You guys, it's time to release the book! It's available now!" The overwhelming rush of emotions overtook me while I was seeing those sales go click click click… I could not believe this was happening so fast! All through baby JESUS! That is what the vision was and now it was happening right in front of me.

It showed me that God can do anything as long as you trust him with all of your heart I was literally witnessing love, respect and favor from strangers. These people did not have a relationship with me and they bought my first shipment within three hours. Funny thing… family and friends were disappointed and kind of upset with me because they did not get a copy. I couldn't save extra copies if I tried! So many people I knew were astounded that the books sold so quickly, and I used to tell them, "Hey, you'd better get on while you can… don't take your time, because this train is moving, and they had to wait for the next printing. See… people sometimes just assume, without even knowing, that they have to catch up with you and you are moving right along. Don't apologize for that either.

A wise woman told me, "Hey, this book is just a business card with legs… you got to work this thing now honey". So that's what I decided to do… work this thing! Interviews started happening and calls were being made. I was traveling to cities to do book signings and it all looked very promising. I was connecting with other authors and influencers, my social media numbers were growing, all was well, at least that's what I thought. I was making more money. Classes were coming from the book. YES!

Wait a minute… what is this? What's this up ahead? What's wrong? Why was this train slowing down and even feel like it's stopping? Not again! Another disappointment… another let down. I am supposed to be moving forward. Why is this happening to us.

Have we derailed? No GOD… please! Another setback? We put our trust in a person who said that they were able to help us go to another level and bam, "God told me to do this and that for you." Turned into "If you don't do it my way you won't get another thing from me!" Oh really. That was a little too controlling… and manipulation was not our plan.

The Truth is…we were deceived again! Clearly I thought that, by now, I was going to be much further along with the book as I'd been promised. I thought that I was going to be all over TV. I thought that I was safe and I could trust. You see promises were made but not kept. This business deal did not work in our favor the way we expected. Why? Because we decided to follow our gut in a situation that brought upon a nasty shift, which brings me to this point. Always do your research about an individual when they are saying what they can do for you. Get everything in writing and ask GOD for greater discernment and wisdom when it comes to all business matters! NO CONTRACT... NO DEAL!

I was the kind of person that people could pull on my heart strings because I was ignorant to the "business" side of life. Oh, I knew the Bible, but when it came to business that wasn't my strength and the devil and his minions knew that! So I would often trust the advice of others even if a had a gut feeling not to do it. I figured, "Hey they been here before and I haven't." Man, did I learn the hard way.

Truth is I chose to listen and respect my husband. Ladies, I did what he asked me to do without a rebuttal, without hesitation or doubt. This time he was right and I needed to obey and submit. I know that word submit is a scary word for those that don't understand what it really means. Why did I do that? My husband needed me to stand for him and value his heart-led opinion.

When I tell you that the backlash from honoring my husband caused friction and tension with this person… to the point where long conversations became short texts, paragraphs in emails became one liners. The spirit of control and manipulation started to pop up and I saw it! Here is the deal… don't tell me you respect marriage and then turn and tell me to disrespect my husband… girl BYE! That's out of order. In spite of the fall out, I couldn't stop what I was doing. Victimization wasn't going to wrap itself around me. The offense was so real. We know that 'offense' is a trap… it's a trick used by the devil to knock us off course, but I had to stay focused. I did what I do best and that's show up on social media and let people know, "Hey, I am here, and I'm NOT going anywhere!"

I did that every day by myself... no distribution... no big name sponsors... no heavy endorsements... no TV... no radio... just Shaun and I, and my will to pursue.

My question to myself was "Did you miss GOD?" Of course I didn't! People have a right to choose and change their minds even if it means they hurt you in the meantime. It's not about you, it's about them! I had to stop blaming myself for having a good heart. God made me this way for a reason. Now I had to learn how to use more wisdom and discernment in business and friendship. I couldn't predict what was to come. Do I look like a psychic or fortune teller? No way. God has a way of making all things work together for our good, because we love him and He loves us.

When people begin to see you climb up, they get a little quiet, as if they feel like you're going to over shadow them or they feel like you're going to outdo them or outshine them. I realize that many people who said they loved me and supported me, that they had my back and wanted to see me win and go as far as the stars, did not really mean it. They really meant "GO AS FAR YOU CAN WITHOUT SURPASSING ME!"

Let me be even more honest. Doubt crept in and I thought to myself, where are you? What did I do to you? What happened? I thought you were going to do this… I thought you were going to open up that door… I thought you were going to introduce me to this person… I paid you to do… you told me you were going to handle this and I made sure I did my part! Why didn't you do your part? The spirit of rejection tapped on my shoulder too and tried to hang around, but that devil be damned! I rebuked those demons chasing me and fought with the word of the Lord! Oh this was so real! Here we go being asked to trust only to be lied to and tricked! There's is no other way to put it. I was ANGRY! God had to keep my mind and my mouth! I wanted to tell the world how we were wronged and hurt, but no, he gave me so much peace. Even in all this, Shaun and I grew closer together. God had to show me that I truly am an entrepreneur and a woman of faith, an inspirational motivator and that I can conquer anything through prayer and through faith and with a support system like none other in my husband. You see, what affects me affects Shaun too. Now I know you're wondering "Did you forgive the person?" Of course we did! You have to release them from having access to your everyday life and sharing with them. I have learned that when you feel dropped, rejected and abandoned that is a great place to stop and ask GOD "What is the lesson in this? What do you want me to see? Father you never rejected me, dropped me or abandoned me. I am not an orphan nor do I have an orphan's spirit. This is not your perfect plan for my life."

It was hard at first… embracing the idea of them not being around and guess what the Lord did… He sent me new friends and people who truly love and support me!

God reminded me to get up… that the matter was in my hands through people who got the real me. I want to encourage you to keep treating people the way you want to be treated, keep loving them in spite of how they stop loving you, keep speaking well of them and supporting them even when it hurts, because God is watching… God is keeping good records… God is seeing how you're handling this storm and offense, and yes, the lies. Listen to me, you have a right to be angry but you don't have a right to stop loving.

He reminded me that he gifted me and that no weapon formed or fashioned against me shall be able to prosper! With tears in my eyes, even as I'm writing this, I want to encourage you to stay strong and not back down! Don't be afraid to do the work… don't be afraid, face your enemies… don't be afraid to persevere even when you're upset… don't be afraid to turn the other cheek sometimes…

don't be afraid to acknowledge that all is well, even when it feels like all is not well... even when it feels like every door is shutting in your face, when all the promises were made and it just seem like everything is crumbling! You still have to smile and push through and nobody knows what's going on in your head... but God does and all is well. I understand now more than ever before that everything is not what it seems and I believe that with this book, God has allowed me to see the unseen and he's allowed me to partake in a conversational relationship just to get me to the place of knowing who I truly am! I'm so glad that God created me to be the Markita D. Collins that I am today and if I did not stand and withstand opposition and pressure I would've broken down during the critical times of the book selling, the book signings, asking people to get the books, and prominent leaders and pastors who said that they were for me and in my corner and they just became ghosts... that's right, they just vanished!

I'M STILL OLD FASHIONED!

You know why I can be "Still Old Fashioned"? It's my husband. He loves me past my flaws. He loves me with no conditions. He loves with no barriers, with no smoking mirrors, without rose-colored glasses. He is truly a man of God… a man of integrity… and I will stand by him no matter what because he stood with me no matter what. He pushed me and continued to make sure that I was encouraged when I didn't want to go on social media and sell books or do classes… I didn't even want to bake. However we had to keep moving, to keep pressing, to keep fighting, and I thank God for the circle of two or three people that really rallied around me during those difficult times to hold me up and to love me through it all. One of those people has gone on to be with the Lord and I'll forever miss him, even as I only knew him less than two years but he spoke some things into my life that I'll never forget. My Grandpa Albert said "Baby, all is well and you're going to go to the top! You and my grandson are going to see things you've never seen before and, if you behave yourself, everything you want God is going to give to you. You don't have to worry about what those people are doing or what they're not doing. Baby, if you just hold on a little while longer you're going to see God move mountains for you, you're going to see it baby. I promise! It's in the master's hand!" God used that man at a pivotal time to warn us and to cover us and to pray for us and to pour into us so much godly wisdom from the old-school era that we needed in this new dispensation… all that this new generation is lacking and I thank the Lord for a friend who stood by us through some of the darkest times. I didn't understand why God would allow all them to see and hear some of the backlash and all the negativity, but they still stood with us as witnesses. One even said "Sis, the devil in cunning and crafty, but y'all are gonna be alright because you and Shaun really love the Lord".

I often wondered to myself what happens when your book is affecting the lives of hundreds and even thousands of people, and from your testimonies, when you come on social media they think you're making all of this money and you're thinking to yourself where is the money? What happens when you have to invest thousands and you don't even have a kitchen table or a couch? Let me tell you it was worth it and more! To be in this place with GOD I would go through this all over again. Hard to believe, but I would.

I've seen miracles, I've seen lives changed, I've seen people go from good to great, I've seen people go from bad to amazing, I've seen people go from loss to gain and it's amazing how my story and my testimony with the wisdom that God gave me in all these chapters transforms the lives of thousands of people.

Thank God for his love. He's taught me how to love people past their pain, he's taught me how to love people past their calamity, he's taught me how to be honest and truthful even when people weren't honest and truthful with me, he's taught me how to be supportive of people and other authors/entrepreneurs, because I wanted people to support and celebrate me. Shaun and I had to celebrate ourselves and be in the moment, live in the moment, put our best foot forward, and be consistent with this process. Listen… everything is not going to come easy. Some things are going to be great and some things not so great, but all things work together for the good of them that love the Lord and are called according to his purpose. Funny thing, I probably would've just given up and thrown in the towel, but guess what? He would've thrown it right back at me! Why? Because God knows the thoughts and plans that He thinks towards us. This wasn't a punishment. No, it was for a greater purpose. Christians go through things just like non-Christians do. No matter how much you pray and fast, we go through things too. So, like David in the Bible, we have to encourage ourselves in the Lord.

Sickness, multiple surgeries, death, family drama, court dates, baby mama drama, bills on top of bills, severing ties, and connections to discern who is a friend, who is an enemy, who is a wolf in sheep's clothing, who's attacking us and who's not.

There's some highs and some lows from the beginning of the old book to the releasing of this new book and I thank God that you are all going to be able to travel with me even in this is a different mindset. I have some more challenges ahead but I have some even greater victories ahead of me as well! We are going to be triumphant! I'm so grateful to God that I didn't give up and I kept my head up. I'm so grateful to God for every buyer, for every person that interviewed me, for every person who has supported me, and I thank God for the people who don't even know my name yet but they sure will because my name is Markita D. Collins and I'm still a wife! I'm not going anywhere! I'm a mother of four amazing children and a dynamic stepmother and I'm a woman of faith and growing in ministry every day! I'm an entrepreneur and I won't hide from the world that I am doing great things. I am a certified life coach, yes me! I am an author of a best-selling international book already and I thank the Lord that he is taking me from faith to faith to glory to glory, continuing on this journey with me… there are some new things in here that are not what you have heard before.

For me, people who were closest to this project tried their best to sabotage us. To literally derail us. God had another plan. A way of escape. A ram in the bush and we just moved on. Ok. There it is. We can feel the train moving again. This time we are not looking back. We are not going to feel sorry for ourselves. This is the thing. You can either get mad, not forgive and seek revenge or you can believe that it's all working together for your good. I feel that train going faster. Yes, we have stops and delays, yet without a doubt, this train is moving, and nobody can stop it!

Let me encourage you… life can be a trip, people can shift and change on you. It feels like betrayal, it feels like a knife in your face not just your back. Honey, persevere, because the best way to prove the doubters wrong is to live your life out loud! The ones that counted you out. Oh and for the ones that deliberately dropped you on the tracks just so the train can run you over... I have news for you. It won't work! No way will it work. Choo Choo let's go.

3 REAL. RAW. UNKUT!

Whew those first two chapters were something else, huh? Well... as you know, I am Markita D. Collins, formerly Markita D. Birden. I'm the eldest of three daughters of Richard and Linda Birden, born and raised in upstate New York. I have been singing since the age of four, and serving in ministry for just as long. I was educated in Catholic and public schools.

Growing up, all I knew was church and family. We were a family of love. There were always big dinners for Thanksgiving, Christmas and birthdays... Sunday dinners and card games after church. Yes, that was a good life!

I saw a lot of love between my parents. I saw them holding hands, hugging and kissing each other. They were really connected. While there was an electrifying unity, they sometimes disagreed, but even then there was a loving connection between them. No abuse and no disrespect where deal breakers came into play. They communicated and it was healthy communication. It's fair to say my parents were a great example of a good marriage.

My father, a hard-working man who wanted the best for his girls. He wanted us to have the best, nothing second-rate. My mother, a beautiful woman, was always giving, serving and helping others. You must understand… my parents came up from the bottom. Hard living! Big families, yep, but not a lot of money. So they provided an excellent life for their girls. My sisters and I didn't know what struggle was really all about. If times were rough, we did not know it!

This wasn't a great time. I remember when my mother didn't want to go to church anymore because of the offense she went through with people in the church. She just couldn't take it anymore, she had had enough. Even then, my father made sure my sisters and I were at Sunday school every week at 9 a.m.

As a child, I wanted to be like my mother and aunts. Lord knows they could sing! Singing to the glory of God until they sang down heaven was an absolute delight. Every time they chorused, the Holy Ghost would move through the church. Now mind you, we were Baptist… violent praisers, lol. They called it the "Baptist fit" and people all around the sanctuary would be touched, healed and delivered as the Spirit of God moved among them as my Grandfather, who was the Pastor, would preach and sing. As I got older, I realized I had the same gift of song. I would sing and people would just fall out under the Holy Spirit.

As much as I had family that loved and adored me, I also had family members that were mean, jealous and insecure, and didn't really love me like I thought they did. They talked about me, lied, gossiped and bullied me. It was a horrible experience that colored my perspectives and beliefs about life, people and myself. For some reason, it was easier for me to believe the noisy, big-mouthed devil than it was to believe the still, small voice of the Spirit of God.

I was picked on at a young age because I was a braces wearing, dark, chubby girl with a funky Jheri curl and a ring around my nose. I was pushed around so much that I would just cry every day. I wanted desperately to fit in. I wanted somebody to accept me for who I was and just like me for being me.

My desire to be accepted and approved of seemed to know no bounds. I made some bad decisions in my pre-teens because I wanted to be down with the "in" crowd. I used to steal candy from stores and cut up in class just trying to look so cool with my friends. At the time, I didn't realize they didn't know who they were either and that's why they did the things they did. They were just like me– lost and looking for ways to fit in. Being bullied forced me to learn how to fight, and that's how I got noticed. I got all kinds of attention, adoration and respect when I finally stood up for myself.

I thank God for those childhood moments. It made me realize that no matter what people did to me, I still had to treat them with respect and let go of grudges. This prepared me for dating young men. Skip to high school, where I wanted to be in love. I was so young and silly! I fell and I fell hard. I gave my heart and my body to people who didn't earn or deserve it. I wish I had waited, but I so desperately wanted to fit in. I was coming from a deep place of rejection. When you feel rejection, the enemy doesn't want you to believe that you are approved and loved by GOD. I believed in God but didn't "believe" Him. At that time I didn't know who I was and so I conformed to what others said who I was. I again wanted to be down with this image of being chosen by a great guy. These dudes didn't know who they were. We were kids trying to be grown-ups. We were not ready for love. What I now know is that it is demeaning to your soul and lasts longer than the few minutes spent exchanging your virtue. It wasn't worth it at all. Hell NO!

I am Markita! Being funny, talented and encouraging made me very popular in high school. It was a hiding place for me. I got along with faculty, staff and students. But then I started to notice that I couldn't get away with anything. I always got caught! I came to believe that it was the Lord's way of course-correcting me and showing me that I was special, gifted and anointed. At the time though, I was still dipping and leaning into wrongdoing. Oh, but GOD shined the light on me... the things my friends did and got away with, I never did. Looking back I realize it was for my good.

Prince Charming... yeah right!

It was my last year of high school and I met this guy my cousin introduced me too. We met for the first time at church on an Easter Sunday. We immediately connected that day. I knew he had to be the one because I was home and a got a knock on the bedroom from my mother. "Hey Kita, a gentleman just asked your father and I if he can escort you to the movies and dinner. So get up child and go!" Oh my word! He called my parents, what a swell fella! We went to the movies and baby, he held my hand the whole time, what? From then on, we were stuck like glue. We were on the phone for hours a day and it showed on my parent's phone bill. I saw no wrong in him. Everybody loved this man. He bought me expensive gifts and spoiled me rotten. He took me to my prom. He would drive from his base every weekend to see me and spend time with my family. He was in with everybody. After high school, and a year of college, he was being sent off to another assignment. Oh, by the way… he was a Sgt. in the military. He was strong and oh, so handsome. We got engaged. He moved to "HOT LANTA" Atlanta, Georgia. We would see each other throughout the year, he would come to visit me or I would go to Atlanta. I thought my life was perfect. It wasn't.

He cheated on me during our relationship even before marriage. He gave me STDs. But he asked me to forgive him and I did... over and over again. I became depressed. I went from a size 12 to a 24. I was the epitome of sadness. There was no joy, peace or satisfaction anywhere in my life. I was pretending to be happy when I really wasn't. I was supposed to be happy because he was an army man, a gentleman, a provider.

Although I was ready to be a wife, he wasn't ready to be a husband. When I look back now, I know he cared about me a great deal and he may have even loved me. But he didn't love me the way God wanted him to love me. And I suffered for that. I went through hell during that time. I got pregnant a couple of times, but I was under so much stress, and so depressed, that I miscarried. I asked God to show me what was going on and I found proof that my husband was sleeping with other women.

Underwear, letters, condoms, pictures. Yep it was all there right in my face the whole time. I was so hurt.

As Maya Angelou said, "When somebody shows you who they are, believe them." He had shown me the truth about who he was; I just couldn't accept it. Never ever ask GOD to show you and you not be ready for the truth.

Though I was faithful and did right by him, in 2003 he wanted out of the marriage. He told me this over an email! Can you believe it? What did I do to deserve this? I was faithful. I did right by you! Why couldn't you just love me the way that God expected you to love me? Why was that so hard? His mother couldn't stand me and she always meddled in our lives. She had the nerve to call me and say "Just sign the papers, he don't want you no more." I told her "I'm sure if you could have him you would be with your own son!" I had enough of her. My skin wasn't light enough. I wasn't thin enough for her son. Ironically all the women in his family except his sisters were thick and heavy though. Did I miss something?

We got divorced and it was the worst feeling in the world. It felt like death. I was dying on the inside. He left me with nothing. He took my name off of all the accounts, broke the $900 a month lease and back then that was a lot for rent in Atlanta. I had to put all my furniture into storage. All I had left was the car, my clothes, and a TV. I stayed in hotels, maxed out credit cards, and stayed with friends who ended up getting tired of me. I even slept in my car for a few days. I remember the last time I saw him, we stayed at a hotel and he asked me to wait for him and not move on, he had to get his head on straight. Was I a fool or what? I believed him. Finally I had to face the music and let my family know I had to come back home.

I packed my car with clothes and other belongings including "The Box" of stuff that he had given me. With a box of tissues on the passenger seat and gospel in the CD player, I drove 17 hours by myself with only enough money for food to get me home.

I was never suicidal, but I was really depressed, and I wanted to kill him for what he did to me. I wanted him to be exposed and suffer. I found out while I was driving in the car that our divorce was final. He destroyed my character. He destroyed me, or it sure felt like it. He mentally abused me. He lied to me. Emotionally abused me. And even physically put his hands on me. He completely disrespected me.

I was devastated. I was humiliated that this person had chosen me, told me he loved me, asked for my hand in marriage, then unceremoniously dropped me. I went to church months prior to all of this happening and spoke to one of the Elders. She was a Prophetess as well. We met in her office and she told me all of this was going to happen. She said that I would be hurt and that I would go through divorce and that was GOD's way of protecting me. That my ex would come to himself but it will be too late and that I will love again and remarry… just not to him. I didn't want to hear that! I wanted my marriage back. She was right and it was over. As time went on I hid in the church but got angry at God and I didn't want to be part of any church anymore, so I went into the world. I found what I thought was a refuge in clubs and drinking and being with men. I thought, "I'm going to get that fool back for what he did to me." But I was hurting myself, not him, and the enemy knew it. I had to pull myself together and have a one-on-one with God and say, "Why did you allow me to go through this? I'm hurt. And I'm angry. I'm upset. I didn't deserve this."

After my time with the Lord, one of my aunts sat with me and prayed over me and counseled me and I had to really give up a lot. Eventually, I went to this church that operated in deliverance ministry. They especially seemed to reach women that were broken. I went there and I gave my all to this church.

Even with all of this support, I was still dealing with the ex-husband, allowing him to come in and out of my life through emails and phone calls. I would get my hopes up, just to be let down again. I had a strong attachment or what people like to say "soul tie" to him. I wanted marriage… not him, it was idolatry because I wanted that more than I did GOD (deep right?). It was so strong and it really messed me up. I did not know how to let go.

A couple of years later, I ended up dating a man who I had known from my past. He told me he was divorced, when in fact he was still very much married and his wife was still very much in love with him. I know that feeling because I was cheated on. Why would I be with a man that's cheating on his wife? I wanted to let go, but I didn't know how.

He told me he was going to leave her. Told me that he had left her and was going to officially get a divorce so he and I could move on. I brought him into my world completely. I trusted him. And then he raped me. Here I go again being attached to a thing that GOD didn't want me to have. When it's GOD it's all GOD. Not half!

I told my family, but nobody believed me, except my sister Tracy and best friend, you guessed it, Shaun Collins. Tracy had a way of pulling things out of me when I would shut down. She grabbed me and she said, "What's wrong with you, Kita? Something happened to you. Tell me what happened to you. Please. Why are you this way? You're hurting, I know you Kita! Tell me." And I told her. I said, "He raped me. Now I'm pregnant and I don't know what to do." She said, "You've got to tell Mom and Dad."

So I told them. But they didn't believe me, which made me that much angrier. They said I was fornicating willingly, so it probably wasn't rape. Not even my own pastor believed me. Why would I lie about being raped? I didn't understand.

They wanted me to keep the baby, but I just couldn't. I couldn't imagine being with someone that had raped me. He raped me and he would have access to me and this child forever. I aborted the baby. So now I am divorced, an adulterous woman and a murderer. That was a hard place to be in. I asked God to forgive me. And I asked the baby to forgive me. Now the hard part, I had to forgive myself.

I didn't trust anybody, but I was still out there, because deep inside I felt like I needed a man. I just needed the company and the companionship of a man – any man. Honey when I look back I asked myself "GIRL WHAT WERE YOU THINKING?! That one didn't have a job, him over there wasn't your type at all, this dude here was asking you for money, this boy was a weed head and lived with his MAMA!!" hahaha. That's why the bible says FORGET THOSE THINGS THAT ARE BEHIND YOU and PRESS!!!!

I was so blinded by what I thought love was and the need to be loved, that I settled for anything. I even settled for friendships with women who didn't mean me good as well. I just wandered around this thing called life.

Then I became really close to my best friend, Shaun Collins. I had known Shaun since high school. Whenever I needed anything, he was always there for me. Little did I know, he had feelings for me, from way back in 1995! He had always been my friend – he was my best friend. BONUS!! So Shaun had asked me to the prom, yes, my husband now… Shaun… follow along now. We picked out colors and everything. I had to tell him we couldn't go because my boyfriend was going to take me now. I wish I knew then what I know now. He was in love with me, as kids are in high school. He never said a word. I was meant to be at the prom with SHAUN!! Ok, let's get back to the story. One day, finally, Shaun told me how he really felt about me. Honey, he didn't want to be my friend anymore! To be honest I told him how I felt about him. We were in love.

I brought Shaun to church and he gave his life to the Lord after a few times visiting. God changed his heart. Saved Shaun. Filled Shaun with the Holy

Spirit. And we've been rocking and rolling ever since.

We did have a child out of wedlock. Josiah was our firstborn. I was surprised I even got pregnant again because every time I got pregnant before, I lost the babies. I think that was God's way of protecting me. He knew that I was supposed to have children with my husband. I know God has a sense of humor. On our honeymoon, we conceived twin girls.

Now, even in this relationship there has been drama. Family drama, baby-mama drama. We both had trust issues. We both were still broken and discouraged from our past relationships.

I had to learn how to trust men again. I had to learn how to trust my gut again. I had to learn how to trust God again. I had to remember the values my father and my mother instilled in me. I had to remember what the Word of the Lord said about me and that I deserved to be happy, have joy and peace.

Shaun didn't have a lot of money, like my exes.

He didn't have a lot of material things, but one thing he did have was my respect. He had a lot of love to give me. My husband is a hardworking, respectful man who treats me like a queen. When he looks at me I know that I am the only woman in the room. He proved long ago that he is a provider, a protector, a supporter, a lover and a giver. An honorable man. Sounds like a husband to me!

I remember after we got married I was still struggling with trust and anger from my past and Shaun said something to me that "triggered" a memory. It sent me almost seven years back and I went OFF! I was screaming and pacing back and forth like a thunder cat, ready to fight. Shaun ran up on me and grabbed me by my arms and shook me... one good time... lifting me off the floor and said "Girl! Stop it, stop this right now! I am not them! I am not going to let you do this. I am not going to hurt you Kita! You have to trust me babe. I love you girl!"

At that moment something broke and I believed Shaun. I heard what he said and I fell in his arms and cried. I asked him to forgive me. This is a safe place, right GOD? Yes it is. I repented to GOD and asked Him to change my heart about men. I was very honest with Shaun and told him, "I'm still healing... please be patient with me." I learned how to respect men again because of Shaun. Because of Shaun, I finally knew what it felt like to be adored, to be wanted, to be respected. Because of Shaun I didn't mind laying my pride to the side and submitting to him in a godly way. In an awesome way, Shaun proves every day that I made the right decision by letting go of my past and trusting him again. Together, we learned to trust God again.

Our marriage has been tried by fire through the years. Shaun and I have endured issues, sickness and health. Hurt by people in the church. Despised and just dragged by folks for no reason. I went through some of the hardest times with his child's mother who tried to destroy me and come in between us many times and it never worked. That BLENDED DRAMA! I am telling you, this stuff is REAL. All the while, we were loving God and building. He kept us through all of those transitions.

Five children later, including his oldest daughter, we moved from New York to Memphis, Tennessee, from Memphis, Tennessee to southern Pennsylvania.

I started a "Girl Talk with Kita" movement, which is a safe place for women who have gone through the things that I've gone through. I am intentionally being a testimony and a blessing. Now that I'm at this point in my life, I'm finally, finally saying, "I do deserve this life. And I'm still old fashioned."

I still forgive people, and guess what… even when I don't want to. I'm still kind. I'm still loving. I'm still thankful. I'm still Letting go of hurt. I'm still cooking for this family. Yes, I'm still baking cookies. I'm still serving him a glass of water. I'm still being sexy, hey that goes a long way (lol). I still have an opinion but knowing when and where to share that opinion. That's important!

I love Jesus for every trial I've gone through. I love God for every moment in my life and I praise Him every day for this journey that I'm on. I'm healed now. Healed from the abuse emotionally and physically. I am no longer broken. I am better for having gone through what I went through to get here. Now I am bold and victorious. I had to endure all of that to reach this place. I had to go through this to reach the girl who was rejected and didn't need a man but who wants a man. I had to go through all of that to show other women that they can be strong and full of the Word and wisdom and still be tender with her man. I had to go through all of that to be every woman – single, married, divorced, rebellious, with married men, from a dark place, pregnant out of wedlock, promiscuous, rejected, hurt, abused, raped, couldn't get pregnant, aborted a child, stressed, alone, confused, prideful, and finally healed and happy. No woman can say to me, "You don't know what it's like." Yes I do, sister. I've been exactly where you are. And I can show you the way out. Listen to me and I'll get you from the dark, lonely, desperate place to the place of joy in the Lord in your loving husband's arms. Follow my lead. This work is anointed to bless you, to deliver you from hiding behind your own strength and fear. Let's deal with it head on!

The Lord has blessed me with a voice that emanates from my self-identity in Him. Your safe place is in God and in knowing who you are. By the end of this work, you will know that you are not alone. Your identity will shift to one of Conqueror. You will become secure in your identity as a woman with no residue of your past. This is possible for you, because He has done it for me.

You may be nasty and confused like I was, you may have settled like I did, you may be lonely and all together just OVER IT! Well, if you want it to be your day, it can be! I can't promise you that you won't cry, you might even get mad at me for some of the things I say to you. That's ok. Just don't stop reading! Get to the end of the journey with me. Are you ready?

4 UMMM .... THEY LIED!

I would be willing to bet that you have been told many times in your life who you are. We could start with simple definitions according to the roles you play or the relationships in your life. They might include: daughter, sister, friend, cousin, auntie, employee, community member, neighbor and likely many others. Or we could approach this conversation from a place of more personal discussion of the qualities you possess. You may be smart, friendly, outgoing, introverted, private, talkative, thoughtful, introspective, boisterous, and the like. People may have labeled you and said you are just like so and so, you remind them of this person or that person. But have you ever stopped to think about who God says you are? It might be worth more than a passing consideration, especially since He is our creator. Maybe it would be worthwhile to examine what He had in mind when He breathed life into YOU. After all, the purpose of the creation is established through the mind of the Creator.

The bible says that you are:

-       Favored (Proverbs 3)

-       A good thing (Proverbs 18)

-       Chosen (Matthew 22:14)

-       Fearfully and wonderfully made (Psalm 139:14)

-       Strong (Ephesians 6:10)

-       Blessed (Deuteronomy 28:3-14)

-       Wise (James 1:5)

Now I know this may be contrary to everything you've been told about yourself to this point. And I declare this to you now, that it is time to stop believing the lies they told you and the lies you even told yourself. It's time to embrace the Truth. This may be the most challenging thing you face. It's so much easier to believe what we have been told by the world, even when there has been no compelling evidence to support it.

Somebody decided something about us and we agreed. What? What sense does that make? Somebody else, probably with their own stuff going on, they don't even love themselves, they walk in low self-esteem… they decided we were less than and we swallowed it and asked for more. Ladies and gentlemen, I put you on notice, right here and now… it STOPS! No more will we allow the enemy to hoodwink and bamboozle us out of our true and rightful place in God. As my husband would say "ENOUGH!"

Proverbs 18:22: "He who finds a wife finds a treasure and finds favor from the Lord." Think about it. Where is treasure found? In the hidden places. Treasure, that thing of great value, is hidden. It's not easily found. Wives in waiting, you need to know who you are and that you are treasure from the Lord. You are the fragrance of the house. You need to know you are valuable. You are like diamonds, pearls, rubies, sapphires and precious gems. Valuable. Start confirming it by telling yourself, "I am valuable." Come on and say it out loud this time.

When you allow people to tamper with you, lie to you or talk about you, your perceived value depreciates. Like a car as soon as it leaves the lot, it loses its value. When you allow people to buy you and to treat you like an object, you lose your own value. You lose your value, daughter. You lose your value, queen. You lose your value, Woman of God. I declare it right now that you are favored. You are treasure. You are valuable. You now have to teach people how to treat you all over again. See the power in this part is saying "I will learn from this. Not be the victim."

When you don't allow who you are to sink into your spirit, you will believe what everyone else says about you and not what God says about you. You will let anyone fool with you and let them tell you you're not worthy of love and being cherished. That's not just limited to a man either. You need to be clear about friendships as well. It's about knowing who you are and not settling for the okie-dokie. Understand?

I need you to know you are not plastic. Not fake. Not glitter or crushed glass! All sparkle and no substance or value. You're favored. A good thing. A treasure.

Wives – Proverbs 31: the virtuous woman

This is a beautiful scripture about the pricelessness of a godly woman. Here it is from the King James Version: Proverbs 31:10-31:

10 Who can find a virtuous woman? For her price is far above rubies.

11 The heart of her husband doth safely trust in her, so that he shall have no need of spoil.

12 She will do him good and not evil all the days of her life.

13 She seeketh wool, and flax, and worketh willingly with her hands.

14 She is like the merchants' ships; she bringeth her food from afar.

15 She riseth also while it is yet night, and giveth meat to her household, and a portion to her maidens.

16 She considereth a field, and buyeth it: with the fruit of her hands she planteth a vineyard.

17 She girdeth her loins with strength, and strengtheneth her arms.

18 She perceiveth that her merchandise is good: her candle goeth not out by night.

19 She layeth her hands to the spindle, and her hands hold the distaff.

20 She stretcheth out her hand to the poor; yea, she reacheth forth her hands to the needy.

21 She is not afraid of the snow for her household: for all her household are clothed with scarlet.

22 She maketh herself coverings of tapestry; her clothing is silk and purple.

23 Her husband is known in the gates, when he sitteth among the elders of the land.

24 She maketh fine linen, and selleth it; and delivereth girdles unto the merchant.

25 Strength and honour are her clothing; and she shall rejoice in time to come.

26 She openeth her mouth with wisdom; and in her tongue is the law of kindness.

27 She looketh well to the ways of her household, and eateth not the bread of idleness.

28 Her children arise up, and call her blessed; her husband also, and he praiseth her.

29 Many daughters have done virtuously, but thou excellest them all.

30 Favour is deceitful, and beauty is vain: but a woman that feareth the LORD, she shall be praised.

31 Give her of the fruit of her hands; and let her own works praise her in the gates.

Did you read that?

Look at this woman! She is phenomenal! She knows her business. She is a help to her husband. Her husband has full confidence in her. Look at how he regards her. She is trustworthy and has proven herself so. She is not sitting around idle. She's not a nagger. She doesn't appear to have time to nag. She's taking care of everyone including the poor. She brings great ideas. She's not lazy, she's industrious. She's creative and a force to be reckoned with in the marketplace. Where did we get the idea that a stay-at-home mom can just sit on her rear-end all day or just go shopping? A virtuous woman has money. LISTEN!! She's not waiting on her husband to do everything. She's got skills. She can take care of herself and her family if need be. If anything ever happened to my husband, I could get some flour, and sugar and do something to make money. I can flip Kita's Kookies and Treats into a full-time gig and still get the bills paid and the living expenses handled. As long as I have a phone, I will always have money. As long as I have hands, I will always have money. Come on... let me encourage you. Everything you need is in your hands. Without or without a man.

Let me remind you of the woman with oil (2 Kings 4). She was an example of a virtuous woman. She was a widow, a single mother of two sons that were about to be taken into slavery because of debt her husband owed. She didn't hide, she didn't lose her mind, she didn't sell her body or even became a side chick. She went to the prophet and he gave her instructions. She did what he said and was able to not only pay the debt, her sons witnessed her obedience and helped her, she also had enough to live!

The Virtuous Woman, out of her earnings, plants a vineyard. She is a business woman. She takes care of the business of her family. And notice that it says, "Out of her earnings, she plants a vineyard." Out of her earnings. She has more than one business. This woman has multiple streams of concurrent income that she uses to increase her businesses.

She's not out spending every extra dime that comes in on Gucci and Louis, shoes, purses and furs. She's putting the money back into the businesses. Taking the earnings from one to increase another. That's wisdom in business.

Now I want to be clear because I hear you saying to yourself, "I'm not good at business. I can't do all of that." What I know is whether or not you are good in business, there is something you do well. There is something at which you excel. Do it. As long as it is legal and morally appropriate, do it. Do it to the very best of your ability and God will bless the labor of your hands. I just told you everything you need is in your hands. Look down at them now. Speak over your hands. Say this: My hands are blessed. My hands are anointed to create. My hands are not afraid to work. My hands can hold money. My hands are not just for scrolling and clapping. My hands are a powerful weapon and they will be used to the glory of God! Because of your obedience, the Lord will open the heavens, the storehouse of His bounty, to send rain on your land in season, and to bless all the work of your hands (Deuteronomy 28:12)

.Okay, hear me… especially you single ladies! You think that when you get married you have to lose your voice and opinion. Stop choosing with your flesh and start choosing with your faith. You only run into that problem when you chose an insecure man who is not confident in you. That's why it's important for the man to find you. Look again at the regard the husband has for the virtuous woman. Verse 28 says, "Her children arise up, and call her blessed; her husband also, and he praiseth her." He's praising her! Not dogging her out, not abusing her, not threatened by her skills and accomplishments. He's praising her! That is significant with regard to their relationship and consideration of one another. Does that sound like a woman whose husband wants her to keep quiet? Or does he appear to value her opinion and input?

I thank God often for my Shaun, he truly supports and pushes (Praises) me in ministry, business, as a mom and more. He never makes me feel bad for doing what I do.

When you marry the one that God has for you… he will honor and respect your opinion. Marriage brings you into agreement with your husband. The necessary, Godly family structure is this – God first for everyone, husband/wife second, then children, then everybody else. For the marriage to work and be successful, God has to be at the center.

Another thing I want to bring to your attention is that the marriage has to be between two adults. By that I mean, you didn't marry your daddy and he didn't marry his mama. You came together as adults making adult decisions and doing adult things.

Eve was a full grown woman when she was created.

I'M STILL OLD FASHIONED!

We don't know how long Adam was asleep. She was presented to Adam as a full grown woman. Some of you are presenting yourselves to men as babies, toddlers, tweens, it sounds funny but you do it because you don't know who you are. You're looking for your man to be your daddy. He's not!

Eve walked with God too. She spent time with the Lord. Are you? Do you spend more time with social media than you do with God? Are you spending more time with dating sites trying to make it work yourself? A lot of men are especially afraid of African American women. We haven't been taught submission without being walked all over. Too many bitter, angry women are sharing false information about men and relationships. They are speaking their experiences as truth. When in truth they are only sharing their painful experiences. No one would dare minimize their pain. It is real for them. However, it is not Truth with a capital "T." Only God's Truth will stand. And whatever you got from the world as an interpretation of your situation needs to stay in the world. It has no place in your marriage or your relationship. You cannot allow someone else's bitterness and pain to inform your relationship decisions. Never listen to a bitter, angry, broken individual. What they have to say will always carry a negative side effect.

There are some singles who are anointed to speak and teach on marriage. Paul wrote almost a third of the New Testament and he was single. Jesus was single and taught on marriage. I'm not disregarding them. But if you are listening to people who are convincing you not to get married because there's no need to or you can just live together, you need to change the people you are listening to.

When you are with the right man, you don't want anyone else. You need to allow God to change your concept about what a wife is. I'm excited when I look at my husband. I'm happy. I'm full of joy. It doesn't stop men from being attracted to me. Of course, they're attracted to me and my joy. Even more so because I'm happy. They are seeking and want to know that happiness as well.

Stop letting people get into your marriage where they don't belong. No one can talk about my husband. Not even my mom. I don't care what he's done. That's my husband. Keep your mouth off of him. And ladies, what happens in your house between you and your husband should stay in your house. No argument should be shared unless you are in danger or if you are speaking to someone with wisdom who will give you wise counsel. It only taints your family's or friends' opinions of him. So when you fall back in love with him, they're still thinking about the argument. And hear me well… stop sharing how great he is in bed with your best friends, single or married. That's how the mess starts, and suspicions are cast. Then you start thinking everybody wants your man. That's not fair to him. You wouldn't him telling his friends how you love him, right? Protect that man. Keep that sacred place between you and your husband where it belongs.

Now you're going to teach people how to treat you and your spouse in your presence. It comes from knowing who you are and loving yourself. I am a strong woman and I have to have a man that can appreciate that. I need a man who can be a cover for me and where I can be soft and tender without being run over. I can't say it enough, God knew that when he gave me my husband.

Some of you saw your mamas get beaten. And some of you saw your aunties get beaten. So now you have to prove to the world that you're not that girl. That you 'ain't goin' down like that. You're so strong you missed it! You missed the one God prepared for you when you ran over him with your attitude and your bravado. You missed it when you dismissed that quiet, confident soul that approached you. You missed it when you had to prove your strength and importance and couldn't be still long enough for him to touch you. 'Cause you still don't know who you are.

I'M STILL OLD FASHIONED!

Stop being bitter because no one proposed this year. Maybe it's not your year. Stop being stuck. Maybe you gotta get your passport and go somewhere you can be found. Stop recycling the same dudes in your little location. You heard me! Same men in the same area code, heck, the same zip code! Honey go see the world. Travel. Stop looking at the prom picture feeling some kind of way about your high school prom date.

Do you know who you are? My declaration for you:

- You are loved by GOD
- You are fearfully and wonderfully made
- You are a woman of integrity
- You are a treasure in an earthen vessel
- You are beautiful
- You are accepted

Honey whether you're light skinned, dark skinned, natural hair, no hair, Brazilian hair that you bought to sew in or glue in, big eyes, slanted eyes, eye brows, no eye brows, short, tall, skinny, fluffy, flat booty, round booty, no chest, big chest, you are still worthy of a man to find you and be committed to you.

They lied to you. Stop letting TV, these waist trainers, these butt lifters, these lip injections, these popular personalities fool you into thinking you have to be them to be desired. They are not living your life, you are. They are not in your circumstance or situation, you are. You are doing the best you can with what you have and who you are.

This is your journey, not theirs. And to be quite honest a lot of what you see are woman buying love. Their perception of what love is damaging, and they face all the embarrassments and shame publicly. Every single time.

Know who you are in God. Know who God is through you, and nothing shall be impossible unto you. In a time of stillness and quiet contemplation, ask God to show you the way He sees you. You might be amazed at the images He shares.

I'M STILL OLD FASHIONED!

- Images of you as royalty having dominion and power.

- Images of you as precious and chosen.

- Images of you as special.

Images of you as a virtuous woman. Feel it. Embrace it. Walk in it. He never lies to you. This is who you are. Nothing less.

5 SIDE-CHICK! REALLY?

Let me make this announcement. I am married. I am not a mistress. I am not a side piece. I am not with anyone else. I am not dating other men. I don't want anyone else. I am secure in my identity as a woman and as a wife. God removed all residue of me being what I am about to dive into it with you. Side CHICK…Really?

According to urbandictionary.com, the "side-chick" is the other woman, also known as the mistress; a diva that is either a male's wife or a girlfriend who has relations with the male while he is in another relationship. That's the world. Its definition relates to extra-relationships, outside of the primary couple. So let's park here for a second. It has become glorified lately to be the "other woman" and is a sweet deal. Why? Because you don't have to commit but you get "benefits", well in my Maury voice "That's a LIE!". You get NO benefits whatsoever. What you do get is far worse than what you can imagine. You may not see

it now, but it will manifest. It's a stronghold, an attachment, a cycle from which you can't break free. The devil wants you to be deceived by making you believe you're in control, when in fact you are not! So if you just sat up in bed or your eyes got real big... yes honey, I am talking to you! Jesus didn't die for you to be a side chick!

I was talking to the Lord one day and He began to show me with His infinite wisdom where this goes a bit further.

How many of us have been the side-chick, even to our spouse or fiancé? How many of us are second to our husband's job, career, business, step-children,

children, in-laws, mamas, daddies, baby-mamas, even the church!

How many of us have become the other woman? How many of us have come home faithfully, done what we were supposed to do as wives and still wound up as the side-chick? The side-chick doesn't get the accolades of a wife, fiancée or girlfriend. She's just a stand-by. How many of us have stood by being married or in a relationship but feeling single and lonely?

Today is the day of freedom and revelation. God wants to heal you of that. Do you know why? Because some of us have made God our side-chick. Picture it. You come to God only when you want Him. Only when you need something. Only when you are in trouble. Think about it now before you dismiss what I am saying. Do you give your allegiance to God? Do you have compassion for God? Do you even respect Him anymore? Be honest in this moment, friend. You tend to want God when you're in a bad place or you need Him to fix something. Side-chicks are known as fixers and the antidote to an addiction or habit. We have put God in the category of a side-chick. He is Our Father who really loves us. Come on, make up your mind. I remember when I said I don't want to do God like that anymore. I want Him to be the lover of my soul for real. I choose God first not second or third. I want God to know that when I wake up in the morning, I want to make You smile. When I wake up in the morning, I don't want to sound foreign to You. When You hear my voice, I'm not just randomly dialing Your number because no one else is available. That's what side-chicks are. When the girlfriend isn't available, when the wife isn't available, the side-chick is always available. The side-chick drops everything to come see about someone that doesn't even belong to her. The side-chick is borderline prostitute, a high-priced geisha. A side-chick is the woman that will never get the husband. And this is where the deception comes in. But again, how many of us have been the side-chick in the

Spirit? Where we are legally bound to somebody or we are getting ready to walk down the aisle with somebody and we're competing with other things in the way. When are you gonna come to the realization that you don't have to be the side-chick? Even if you are sleeping with someone or being with someone who doesn't belong to you right now! I decree and declare in the name of Jesus you WAKE up and come to yourself, God has so much more for your life.

I have had so many women come to me and say, "I get it Markita. But what you need to understand, Woman of God, is that you lay next to triceps and biceps every night. You have a husband that loves you and you have a family and this and that." And I tell them I know how they feel. I've been there, done that. I was in love with a man that didn't belong to me. I didn't know that he had a wife, that he had a child. But because of flesh and because of abandonment, rejection, lies, lust and because of being out of the will of God, my emotions got all wrapped up and my spirit, my flesh got tangled up in that. I didn't know how to get out of it. I was lost and confused. I knew it was wrong, but my flesh craved what didn't belong to me. I had to cry out to God to get me out of that. I didn't want to be the side-chick. I'm not the wife. I'm not the girlfriend. I'm the other woman. I'm the adulterous woman. I said, "God, I gotta get outta this. What am I doing here? How did I get to this place? I know you didn't have this in mind for my life. I gotta change the way I think. HELP ME GOD! I gotta pack up and move. I gotta get in the car and drive. I do not deserve to be in this mess. I gotta get outta here. 'Cause I'm more than the other woman. I'm more than the side-chick." You see, I was desperate to get out! I didn't want that life with anyone anymore. I didn't even have all the words and the proper vocabulary I just knew "This isn't it GIRL!"

So, what do you do? First, you've got to remember who you are. You are favored. It's your name and a lot of you don't even know what your real name is.

You think your name is Kelly. You think your name is Jackie. Do you really think your name is Helen? Do you really think your name is Tasha? No, my queens, my darlin's, my princesses, my sisters. Your name is "Favored."

When you realize favored is treasured, you will hold yourselves up. You will esteem yourselves in a different way. As I said before, TV reality shows and what you see on social media is not our reality when we're in God. And no, it is not God's intention for you to be bitter and upset and mad because, for some reason, nobody has found you yet. He can't find you because you're with somebody else. Ask God for patience, and to teach you how to wait. Yes, I said it… WAIT on the LORD and WAIT for your HUSBAND! And another thing, stop lying to you and us! If you want to be married in your heart, then embrace that. Stop pretending that you don't want to be in a loving committed marriage due to past relationships. HEAL GIRL! You are self-sabotaging when you speak these lies over yourself. So, repent now and renounce all word curses and vows you made and speak life!

Wives, your husband can't find you because you've allowed yourself to be second to everything else. Tell that man, tell that husband of yours to listen… communicate. This is my next point: communicate with grace and with wisdom and passion. "I love you; I'm in love with you, but listen, we got to spend time together because I feel like I'm in competition with your computer." Quick story. Shaun is a tech guy and he loves anything that has to do with graphics, web design and creating for people. But I felt like I had to make an appointment to spend time with him. Yes, I understood he was grinding, pushing out work and making it happen for us, but there was no balance. I had to communicate to him. "Hey we gotta hold hands and I need you to hold me and cuddle me and go with me for a walk. I need that because I feel like every time your mother calls, work calls, your baby mama calls, the Bishop calls, your clients call, you drop everything for them but you won't drop everything for me. I need you. I need you to be there for me like you're there for the kids. Like you're there for the Pastor." You feel what I am saying ladies?

So, you've got to convey that with passion and with humility. "Listen, I got to get this off of me. I can't be the other woman. I can't be the wife that you treat like the side-chick."

You have to be careful, Wife, that you are not so humble, walking in false humility, that he forgets and starts to take you for granted. Sometimes you gotta remind your husband, "Honey, I'm over here." Listen, because he's so relieved that you're not a nagger and you don't smother him. He's so relieved that you don't bug him about everything. He's so relieved that he can trust you to handle those kids that you did not birth for him. He's so relieved that he doesn't have to worry about you spending all the money. He's so relieved that you're not all over him. Sometimes you get lost in the "Oh that's my girl. She's good over there. I don't gotta worry about her.

She understands." Then you'll internalize that and it will become hidden rejection. Then it will become a fit that will rise up and you'll start noticing how he drops everything for everybody when you feel like he won't drop anything for you. And unless it's addressed in a healthy way between you, it festers and turns into resentment and unresolved anger. The devil wants you to stay in that place, but no more!

You are not the side-chick and I'm telling you what to do to get yourself back in order. Use wisdom. This is not the time to confront him with anger and rejection. Build him up with appreciation and admiration. Assume the best about him and his choices where you are concerned. Avoid believing the worst. Could it be that he is not intentionally overlooking you, forgetting about you? Could it be that you are the only stability in his life right now and he is actually grateful that you are not as needy as the others? Assure him that you're not going anywhere. You have to build that man up. Shower him with praise and reminders that you're still on his side. "Honey, I love you. You're so good to me. You're so kind to me. I appreciate you. Baby, you rock. You're not alone. I got your back. You're not by yourself. You're not holding everything down on your own. But I do need a little hug and a little loving every once in a while. I need you to make love to me, hold me, kiss me on the forehead once in a while. I need that from you. Without me telling you. I want you to treat me how you treated me when you first got me. Remember when you first got me? You wrote me letters and notes and held my hand and you opened the door for me. You courted me. I still need that." You need to let him know how that made you feel. "I remember when you used to do that and it made me feel so good." So, you won't be the side-chick and then resent him. Because you see how eager he is to do for everyone else, while you feel like second fiddle.

To my single ladies who desire to be a wife, here are some hints and tips for you when your husband does find you. When the man does find you, you will know what to say and what to do. What you don't want to say is, "Listen, we're getting married, so you tell yo mama, ya baby mama, ya cousins and all of them that they better get it in line, because I come first. I'm your wife, not them." That never turns out well. Sweetheart, if he's a man of God and he loves the Lord, he understands order and God's family structure. Sometimes you have to remind him of the order. If you have to go into the relationship schooling the man then you got a boy, not a man. But he who findeth a wife findeth a good thing and receives favor from the Lord. God didn't call you to be dealing with a boy that you have to teach and instruct. Adam was a full-grown man. Eve was a full-grown woman.

Who are you with? Are you with somebody that you have to teach and school? Are you with somebody that you gotta constantly remind, "Thus sayeth the Lord?" Did he find you or did you find him? Did you yoke up to the wrong man? Are you having to teach him how to be a man? Being a man is not limited to providing and covering. I want an entire man.

Girlfriend, it's too late in the day to try to figure out if you're with a boy or a man. It's too late in the day to be side-chick to some man who doesn't realize who you are. Let's ask the hard questions. Have we become projects? Have we become the answer? Are we healing the system? Are we getting to the root of some stuff? Because, most often, side-chicks come because there is something that the wife is not fulfilling. It's not fair. And it's not right. Most often the side-chick is doing something that the wife or the fiancée is not doing. Are we affirming our men enough? Are we celebrating our men enough? Are we pushing our men the right way? Are we pulling them to an expected end? Are we pulling them up to the vision? Are we reminding them of the vision? Can we remind them of the vision when they kinda fall off? Are we helping them along the way? Or are we the kind of women that would push our men into the arms of something, or someone, that feels safe, even though it is very dangerous?

Most side-chicks, unless they are really, really bold, don't want to be side-chicks. But she settles because she knows, "I'm giving him something that his wife isn't giving him." That's what she thinks in her mind. But she's delusional. She's thinking, "I'm giving him something that he can't get from her, so he has to get it from me. So, I'm okay being the other woman because then I don't have to obligate myself." Side-chick, you need to get healed, and you need to get delivered. Leave people alone, you lied to yourself. God loves you too, but He doesn't love what you are doing. You've convinced yourself that this is a healthy life and I am here to tell you that it is not.

At the end of the day, God is still God. And He will deal with that man at the appointed time. The wife will deal with the husband. Wives... you never deal with the side-chick. Hear me...wives never deal with the side-chick! You don't come down from the tower, Rapunzel. You stay up there until it's time to come down. You don't deal with people who are trying to attack your marriage, remember we wrestle not against flesh and blood, but against wickedness and rulers in high places. This is a spiritual battle and you must handle it accordingly! You fight in the spirit not in the flesh. You pray and you believe for God to turn this thing around. You tell the devil to take his hands off your marriage and rebuke every attack in Jesus name. You deal with him, you don't deal with her.

See, we weren't taught right. We were taught to fight the girl. And the guy just sits there like, "What's going on?" So girls, you both have been duped again. He did it. Why are you trying to fight another woman when she was duped too? She should have known better, but she was just messed up in her mind. I've been there. Telling myself this is all that I deserve and didn't know how to come up out of it, until the Lord dealt with me. Again, today is your day of freedom. I speak to your mind and heart right now, that you are not bound to a life of being the other woman, God has greater for you! You will not be attached to ungodly relationships and circumstances. In the name of Jesus, fear of being rejected and abandoned is far from you! You are accepted by God and greater is coming.

6 SETTLING .... FOR FOOLS!

Ladies!!! You don't wanna be nobody's wifey and settle. I want you to trust what I have to say regarding this matter and pray this prayer with me: *Father, in the name of Jesus, I praise you and thank you for who you are and what you've done and what you're about to do in my life and in the life of this reader. I pray that you bless, cover, and protect, God, the woman that is changing her mind about who she is, even at this moment. I declare and decree in the name of Jesus that no weapon that is formed against this woman and anyone they are connected to shall prosper. I bless you in advance for uprooting every demonic curse, word curse, lie, habit, false way of thinking and cycles*

NOW in the name of Jesus. Thank you, Lord, for teaching us how to do things the right way, the Wifely Way. Thank you, God, for giving the reader courage and wisdom, knowledge and understanding on how to go to the next level in their marriage, even if they are not married... how to become ladies in waiting and wives. If they're going through divorce, I pray God, that they will forgive, heal and recover quickly. Father, I thank you that you're healing us from the inside out. I thank you that you are truly the lover of our souls and there is no good thing that you will keep from us if we walk uprightly before you. Father, I thank you for every reader that represents favor. I thank you for every reader that represents the kingdom of God. Lord, I thank you for every woman that is going to the next place in you because she trusts the word of this Woman of God. Not only do I believe that you are a curse breaker, but you are the answer for their lives. Thank you for snatching them out of pits and dark places. I give you glory for the turnaround. And I believe with all my heart that you are still Lord and you can't fail. In Jesus' name, Amen.

Listen up, God never wanted you to settle and just be somebody's "wifey." He wanted you to be a

WIFE. What is a wife? Let's look at the definition: a married woman considered in relation to her husband. Synonyms for wife are: spouse, partner, life partner, mate, woman, helpmeet and bride. From a biblical perspective, when God put Adam to sleep and took out his rib he made woman. So, let's not be confused, a wife is a woman or female and there's certain roles and things we are to do as wives that have nothing to do with being a wifey and settling.

Let me ask the question. So, who are you gleaning from? Who taught you how to be a wife? Do you want to be a wife for real? What are some of the examples you have and the lessons that you've learned? Who have you surrounded yourself with? Are you reading the Word of God? Are you studying people? Do you find yourself looking at TV? What was your idea of marriage? Now what is your idea of being a wifey? Do you think it is the same thing as being a wife? Do you think that God wants you to waste years and years of your life and time waiting on somebody to finally realize who you are and choose to marry you? Are you limiting yourself to greater possibilities? Are you settling right now? Are you giving your body up to someone who doesn't belong to you, who keeps promising that he will marry you? Do you have the stamina to stand and wait? Or are you too afraid to walk away? Be honest with yourself now. Nobody is around to judge you. It's just you, these words and GOD right now. Are you in a relationship that you know is not healthy and you know God wants you to leave that relationship, but you don't know what else to do? So instead of being a wife, you settled for being a wifey. What are some of the things you're doing? How are you preparing yourself? What are you saying to yourself? What are you really thinking at this moment?

At this point in the game, what we know is that we have value and worth. We also know that God never made us the side-chick. We are going to learn now that being a wifey, a live-in girlfriend, or someone waiting on him to make up his mind is also not what God intended. Now the question you must ask yourself is "Am I willing to let it all go and wait for someone that God wants me to be with, or do I choose to settle and be foolish because I'm afraid to release and let go?"

Take a deep breath. I know that was hard.

Statistics say that nowadays most marriages last from three to eight years. Statistics say that usually people whose relationships end in divorce get married two to three years later. Statistics also say that the longer you date, the longer your marriage. These are the world's systems. I believe that as a Woman of God, God has a system for us. And we need to do things the way God wants us to do them. For some people you may go right into courtship and get married. For others dating, courting and then marriage. I have even seen people get married after only knowing each other for a few months and they are married for years!

If we learn the principles of what dating,

courting, engagement and marriage are, we would not go through this revolving door of marriage. If we stop confusing dating and engagement, and courting and marriage, we would not be in these situations where we are constantly turning over relationships. Stop giving away your territory to people who shouldn't have free reign in your life. "Here's the key to my house. Here's the key to my car. Come move with me. Come stay with me."

Real quick… If you know that you want to be a wife and no longer settle speak this right now: I am a WIFE and I want the husband that GOD has for me! Why did I have you do that? Because your words have power! Life and death as we know is in the power of your words. Ok let's move on.

Do you know the difference between dating, courting, engagement and marriage? And for the wives reading this, you need to know that there are still things you need to learn as a wife. Have you been tricked into thinking that your way is the greatest way? As a wife you need to know that you can grow and flourish in your marriage too. Do not settle for what worked 10, 20, 3, or even 6 years ago. Are you up for learning how to change the way you perceive things? Are you up for the challenge of asking God to show you where you might have stepped off the track? Are you willing to hear how to strengthen your marriage, and how to be more of an aid to your marriage instead of a hindrance? Do you believe you're doing all the things that you're supposed to do in your marriage? I have some miserable wives that make "Wifeys" feel they are better off settling because how your life looks.

Hmmmm… quite frankly being a wifey is a disrespect to you. There's no honor in that at all. I know and understand that it is a trendy word and it sounds real cute. It's on t-shirts, magnets, mugs, heck people blog about it! I'm not coming for anyone or knocking what others may think a "wifey" is, but there's nothing cute about being a "wifey"! Wifeys never become the wives. Did you hear (read) what I just said? Wifeys do everything the wife does but she does not get the ring. It might be a ring, but a not a wedding ring… not a covenant. She doesn't get the claim. She doesn't get to say, "I am his wife." She doesn't get to have his last name. She doesn't get to have the things legally that a wife does. Now I am talking from a Christian lifestyle not the world. I want to be clear about that. She doesn't get to say she was found. She doesn't get to walk around proudly and declare that she is his beloved, that she is his good thing. She does not have the luxury of any of that. All she can say is that "Hey I love him. We live together, and it works out for us." In her mind, she has accepted that "This is all that I can get." She has decided that this is the only way to be with someone and has become okay with it. In reality, the wifey is never okay with it. She's just too scared to detach and let go of whatever connection she thinks she has. So, she allows the disrespect to pile on and lets the years go by. Settling.

Then there are children. They may be able to have the father's last name but she'll never have it.

Or ten or twelve years later, he decides to marry her. All those years wasted, waiting to be chosen. It breaks my heart when I see this. Settling. There are too many people telling the wifey not to mess up a good thing. "Girl, don't rush him, don't put pressure on him." Wait a minute here. After 5 years, he still doesn't know if he can commit? Nah!!!! A man, not a boy, knows who his wife is, he is not going to string her along and play games. He is confident and not ashamed to declare his love openly to the world about who he found. Maybe she didn't know because her judgement is cloudy and the people around her won't tell her that she deserves better than that. She deserves to be respected.

Let me throw this out here too. Maybe the problem is that he doesn't know how to be a husband. Maybe he never had the role models he needed to know how to respect you. Maybe he wasn't taught properly... not that it is your job to teach him. Maybe he doesn't know how to court you, how to love you, how to not put you last.

Maybe he didn't know that he had to come in with vision. Maybe he didn't know that he had to make a decision to choose you and leave everybody else alone and move forward versus hanging on to his past of whatever it was he saw. Maybe he didn't have a male figure telling him how to treat a woman and how to be a man... what you do for a lady. Maybe he just plain didn't know.

But ladies, even if he doesn't know, you should. You should know the difference between being a wifey, a "Booh" and a "Bae," and a wife. I have been there! I know. Ok here we go... "Story time"... I love giving my testimony because I know it's going to help you! Shaun literally broke a generational curse off his bloodline. He grew up where it was an honor to be a baby daddy and not get married. The men he admired and was influenced by were not committed to one woman, some lived with women, raised kids together yet would not take it to the level of covenant. When he and I decided to be together I knew I wasn't going to settle for just being his lady and baby mother. I didn't make him choose me, I chose me! That life wasn't an option for me. We had a rough time during my pregnancy, he wasn't even happy at first that I was pregnant (Like I did that by myself!). We went through so much, though we knew we loved each other, there were cycles we were fighting. Because of our choices even while being saved, we suffered consequences for them. I didn't think we were going to make it. Shaun had a baby mama already and I wasn't competing with her, his mother, or his child. I was fully prepared to be his other baby mama because I refused to settle. Well we had a huge fight and my aunt wanted to meet with us. She looked at us and said "NOW WHAT IS THIS?" She had a way of just getting to the root! I said "Hey if he doesn't want me, I don't want him! I am not waiting around for him to see that I am the best thing, besides Jesus, that ever happened to him." Of course, my aunt looked at me and said "Kita, shut up! All of this is foolishness and the devil is trying to keep you two from coming together and it's working." She is 5'4", Shaun is 6'2", and she got in his face and said "Now what do you think you're doing here? Your son is watching you." I was 7 months pregnant with our son at the time. And when she said that he started kicking and flipping in my belly. She said, "That's right! Josiah is looking for you to break the cycle son." We still had hurdles and it was just hard. Moving on to me going into labor… I promise you it was so scary and long, but when our son was born it was as if something broke off Shaun and I. He looked at me as I was pushing and telling me how much he loved me and he was proud of me. When I held our baby we both cried, Shaun said "You did it babe, look what you did." All the while our son was looking up at us and the way God swept through the room was priceless. Shaun proposed to me Christmas day at midnight. Six months later, I walked down the aisle and my father gave me away again. This time it was the last time. This was the will of the Lord and we didn't allow cycles to keep us out of it!

You see, queens, we have totally changed the structure of God's kingdom. We are okay with living with somebody first, having their babies, and then getting engaged then getting married. That is so backwards! Does it work for some people, yes, but is it still backwards? YES! We are so okay with having someone live with us for three and four years, sleep with them, cohabitate with them, do everything together and then maybe we'll get married or maybe we won't. We have become so comfortable with sin that when somebody is doing it right, we consider it strange. We've gotten so used to dysfunction that we think it's normal. This should not be normal anymore. I pray that even as you're reading this that you are not offended. But that there is a stirring in your belly, that you feel a tangible wind as a sign to you that yes GOD is speaking right now. Don't get use to brokenness. Don't wear it as badge of honor. It stops here.

Check this out. To qualify for a gastric by-pass surgery, you have to be a certain weight. To get the surgery to help you lose weight, you must weigh a certain weight. The doctors have made it so desirous to have this surgery, that people are gorging themselves to gain the weight to get the surgery to lose the weight. That's crazy. That's dysfunction. Why does that make sense? Sure, sometimes people need extreme help to lose weight, like I did! I had a VSG (Vertical Sleeve Gastrectomy). It was the best decision for me and I don't regret it at all. Some others just need to fall back to the basics that still work and are healthy. Exercise, eat less sugar and carbs, eat more fiber and green vegetables, drink water and lots of it.

That same theory goes for relationships. Stop doing what everybody else is doing just because it's become the common way of doing things. Stop putting everything in your name – phone, credit cards, cable, loans, car payment, the house or apartment, the utilities. You're buying all the groceries, letting him sleep in your bed. He helps "when he can." You're having his babies and hoping he's going to marry you someday, being loyal to an idea, but seeing this reality that you have settled. Hoping someday he'll see your worth and choose you above all others. How can he see it if you don't?

God never wanted that for you. He does not want you to be around someone who is just a baby-layer and a user. Now hold up! I am not dragging men. Some of you women manipulated the situation because you laid there too! Yes, you did, and it never worked to your advantage and now you are paying for it. You are a part of this too now. I just needed to say that. You can't always blame him. Take some responsibility in this thing sis!

Consider this, when you are a wifey he can just come and go as he pleases. There's no real commitment. Why would you believe or expect that God would not want you to be married? Why do you believe you have to help God by living out of order, just to have a man? Who lied to you? You don't know if he's going to choose you or not. I have worked with women who were with a man many years without being married. He fell out of love with her, left and was married within the next year. Do you know how devastating that is for a woman? "You spent all that time with me when you didn't have nothin', living off of my income and my resources. When you didn't have anything, I was your everything." I hear these stories all the time. I always ask the question "Did you limit yourself to being that man's wifey? Why did you settle?" It's a disrespect to who you really are. And if you have been through divorce, you don't have to rush into marriage. You need to heal. Heal and take your time. It does not mean that you'll never be married again.

I was divorced and now I'm married to an amazing man. I'm happier than I ever imagined possible. When God does a thing, He does it so well. There are times I literally forget about what I've endured. And the only reason that I discuss what I've been through is to help someone else with my testimony. As you've been reading, I am sharing stories and my testimony to encourage you. Listen love, you're not the only one going through. You're not alone out here! I share to help bring someone else out of their dark places. Otherwise I wouldn't have anything to complain about. Let me tell you something My husband is good to me. He was sent by God to find me. He knew I wasn't his wifey though the devil tried it. He knew I wasn't his "girl." He knew I wasn't just his honey. He knew I was his wife, his good thing. Thank you Jesus! Shaun came to himself!

Those of you who are married have an assignment. You are to help your husband meet the goal, manifest the vision, help keep him on task, bring things to his remembrance. I just described the role of wife or "helpmeet".

You've got to make sure this man is focused. Sure, you want to be attractive to him. You want to stay desirable for him. But your responsibility to your husband goes further than that. You must be an aid to him, to remind him of the call on his life.

You don't do all of that for your boyfriend or your significant other. Why should you? What's the commitment? Reserve that for your husband. Care about your boyfriend all day long, but don't be a wifey. Why should he buy the cow when he can get the milk for free? Think about it. Why should he marry you when you are already giving him everything that a wife would give him? I am not saying that you play the "I don't think so because I'm not your wife," games. You should never be petty. But you've been with someone for some three or four or five or ten or twenty or thirty years, it's past time for a decision to be made. It's time for HOLY matrimony to take place. And let me be clear, there are some who are married and it isn't holy. It was not created by God. God never told them to get married to that person. So those marriages were not ordained by God. He honors them because He honors the covenant, whether He was in it or not. When He sees marriage, He sees a covenant.

I'M STILL OLD FASHIONED!

You don't have time to play games and play house. You don't have time to test the waters to see what it's like to live with him. To be honest most can't cohabitate with the opposite sex, unless it's a relative or roommate. The majority of us would sleep with them. I have a cousin who's been engaged for the last thousand years. She and her fiancé live in a two-bedroom apartment together. All the while she's telling us they're waiting to get married and he sleeps in his room and she sleeps in her room. Huh. Well guess who's pregnant? I know another woman who moved in with her boyfriend, two kids later he's in love with another woman and leaves her and the kids. All I'm saying is that We just can't do it y'all.

Why are we settling? Do you know people are teaching classes on how to be a wifey? They're actually teaching people how to stay in bondage. They're teaching people that God doesn't have to design our relationship; we can do it ourselves. They're teaching people how to accept that they may never get his name. I am standing with you girl!

WAKE UP! Shake yourself! Snap outta it! This is not the plan He has for you. I don't care what they say!

The message is that I have his body, his children and his "respect" and I'm happy with that. I know people in their fifties, sixties and seventies who are just now getting married to their "baby-daddy." They lived together twenty and thirty years. The kids are in college and they are just getting married. Why didn't anyone tell these ladies they should be married? They should not just accept that they're living together and it works. He does his thing, she does her thing. What about medical insurance? What about bankruptcy? What about legacy? What about LIFE?!

God will give you a way and a strategy to handle all of that. Do you think we're talking about a God that can't fix your credit? That can't get you out of bankruptcy? Do you think we're talking about a God that can't help you out of legal situations? Do you think we're talking about a God that can't work it out for you? Come on! Don't you believe the God of the Bible you read? Don't you believe your Father in heaven will take care of you better than any person? Don't you believe the God that you pray to that makes this stuff right?

Don't ever, EVER settle for being somebody's wifey when God said your name is Favor. How can your name be Favor if he doesn't marry you? How can your name be Favor if he doesn't find you and choose you for the long haul? You deserve it. Why would you ever make it okay in your mind, "Well this is what it is and I'm okay with it." You should not be okay with that. Something ought to be stirring up in you right now telling you that you deserve more than that.

This is no shade to men because I believe this generation has not been taught. I'm talking about this generation, honey… this forty and under crew. They are different. They don't understand the biblical principles. They think it's "old fashioned." You know what, though? It has order and it has structure and there is nothing corny about doing it

God's way. You're blessed when you do it God's way. You're blessed when you do what God says. You shouldn't want to be a statistic. You shouldn't want to be the one who stays married for two years after living together for twenty. Do you know that God is obligated to bless you when you do it His way? He's obligated to bless you. Receive that word! God said that he is a man of His word. He cannot lie! He is going to bless those that obey him.

You can't do it the world's way and expect to be blessed. The world will tell you that it's okay to masturbate and touch yourself. God says, "That is not Me, I'm not in that." The world says it's healthy. The world says you're releasing toxins and pheromones. What about what God says? He wants your bed to be pure. He doesn't want gates to open that should be closed. He has a plan for you! You have to believe the Word of God. His methods are always right.

You do not deserve to be chosen last, queen. You do not deserve to be waiting for someone to realize who you are and waiting for someone to pick you and to see your value. You deserve more than holding him down and being his ride or die chick. You deserve to have that man's last name. You deserve to have him honor you, protect you and cover you the right way. And if he can't do that then you've got no business with him and he has no business with you!

The only reason you are with a man that isn't doing all of that is because you've been deceived, lied to. I get it, you're scared, lonely and horny. Scared of being alone. Your body is craving. And if he walks away, you're asking yourself, "What will I do? I have these kids. What will I do? Am I going to work another job? Am I going to have to get government assistance? Am I going to have to move back in with my parents?" You cannot allow fear to keep you so captive that you don't believe God to turn it around for you.

So I prophesy to you right now: The spirit of fear is being broken off your life right now! Ungodly cycles and patterns are being destroyed! I prophesy that you are not stuck or bound to attachments, strongholds and curses! I decree and declare that God our Father gives you wisdom, courage to stand, strength to endure.

Some of you will be rejected. You'll have to make some decisions and it's gonna hurt your feelings. And you're not going to understand why you're going through what you're going through. But on the other side of this, I decree and declare that it will make sense to you. I decree and declare that your latter will be greater than your now and your past. I decree and declare in the name of Jesus, that you will not be held captive by being limited in your marital status. That you will not be bounced around. That you will not feel the drop. That you will not be embarrassed. That you will not be ashamed to walk away. But that you will have the poise of a woman. You will have poise and grace and be dignified. You will stand on the promises of Jesus! You will stand on the word and not be moved. You will not accept anything less because you are a wife. You are nobody's wifey, you're nobody's sex toy. Nobody's play thing. Nobody's guessing game… do I want you or not? Nobody's sleeping-over buddy.

Nobody's baby-layer. Nobody's baby-mama. You're a wife… not just any kinda wife either, a powerful wife, a wife who is confident. And as a wife, I speak into your life, you will do things the wifely way. Honor that man, you will cover that man in prayer, you will honor him as your husband. It is not hard for you to shut your mouth and listen. You will trust your husband. You will not be afraid to submit. It is not hard to come into agreement with him. I declare that you have the strength to endure. I believe God is giving you the grace and the patience to work this stuff out. Because He never intended you to settle for a fool.

I think to myself when I see these ladies who have given their lives away and settled for being the wifey, how tragic it is that she doesn't know who she is. If she did she would never put up with that nonsense. She would never settle for that mess. You have to know the power you have as a wife. You have to know the influence you have. You have to know how the enemy hates you and wants you to be depressed and dealing with low self-esteem. He wants you to think you're too bossy, too arrogant. He wants you to think there is something wrong with you. He wants you to think you'll never get out the cycle. He wants you to think there is no hope for you. As a man thinketh so is he. If you are not thinking on the things of God then you're focused on the things of the world. God is saying you're a wife but you keep hearing wifey. God keeps saying your name is Favor and you keep hearing "not good enough." You are a woman of God. You are a wife. I celebrate you now. You're starting to believe it, re-read this chapter if you have to. All is not lost. You can learn from this and walk in the life of a WIFE!

7 SIZE DOESN'T MATTER

Ok I know exactly where your head went when I said that. But we are about to hit a lot of angles for this. Relax, I'm going there, let me just make this very clear. You will miss the God-intended opportunity to be with an amazing man of God by doing the following things. Brace yourself sis!

- Lying to yourself
- Not discerning
- Not having a prayer life
- Having unreal expectations
- Being mean and passive

  Comparing him to your past

Comparing him to other men that have money
or a lack thereof

Comparing him to your friends boyfriends or
husbands

Comparing his size (You know exactly what I
mean!)

Comparing ring sizes

And comparing your life to somebody else's life
Let me say this: What God has for you, queen, is
definitely for you... specifically for you. Meaning that
when God created you, He knew specifically who
He wanted you to be with. A lot of times we fall out
of the will of God. We fall definitely for you...
specifically for you. Meaning that when God created
you, He knew specifically who He wanted you to be
with. A lot of times we fall out of the will of God.
We fall out of the perfect will of God and we go
into
the permissive realm. You just read my story! We
start trying to make things happen spending time
with people we have no business dealing with.

I'M STILL OLD FASHIONED!

Now let me tell you this: dating is fine. There's nothing wrong with dating. Dating is just an activity. It's like a sport.

We're collecting data. It's the "introduction stage." Dating is not me falling in love and being intimate. You want to get to know me and I want to get to know you. A problem arises when we get dating confused with courting and engagement and marriage. We start sleeping with people that God never intended us to have a relationship with… ever. We start making decisions with our flesh, which is weak then we have all these attachments and can't let go of images that are in our minds.

If your memory allows you, think of all the men you've been with. Hopefully there have not been many, but if so, no condemnation… trust me, I am not here to hurt you, and when I say be with I don't just mean sexually, but mentally and emotionally too. Ok just think of them. Think of all the people you let come into your life, come into your spirit, come into your space and literally come inside of you. God never intended that for you or me!

Now, because we have information we were never intended to have in the first place, we compare sizes of men and you're married to Billy but you keep thinking about Keith, how Keith used to do ya. I have been there! Many times, outside of the will of God, we begin to compare one to another. He's not big enough. His car isn't big enough. His bank account isn't big enough. His goals aren't big enough. His degrees aren't big enough. His penis isn't big enough. His tongue, his hands, his height, his weight, his feet, his nothing is big enough.

Meanwhile, God is saying He has the one for you. Remember your name is Favor. He didn't create you to be a tester. He didn't call you to figure this out. He doesn't require that of us. He didn't intend for you to experiment to find the answer. He really doesn't need your help sis. He created you to be the hidden treasure. How are you hidden if you are out trying to find him yourself? Seriously, we need to stop playing God in this. Remember GOD doesn't need our help. He is God and God alone. At the end of the day you're an adult and can make your own choices but, and I do mean but, if I see you on your knee proposing to a man, honey I am going to tap you on your shoulder and say "GIRL GET UP!!!!"

To the marrieds... be honest, if you have men in your head that do not belong to you it's time to get rid of them. Do you realize that unless you've been delivered and set free from your past, you are literally laying down with your husband comparing him to the men and some of you even women you've been with before him? That means that you have not divorced or let go of their size. As long as you hold on to those memories, your husband never measures up or stand a fighting chance for the real first place in your heart. And the real deal is that their size doesn't and cannot matter when you are with your God-given husband. So... Let it go!

Don't get caught up with wanting to be familiar with the anatomy of another man – his body, his bank, his life and what he has to offer you – that you miss the divine connection between you and the one God wants you to be with. See the devil sends familiar spirits to us on purpose. You have a right to be free from them! This is not about who you think you want to be with. This is completely about who God has for you. The wedding vows say, "What God has put together, let no man put asunder." That includes the man in your head, sis. You can't afford to get caught up with the fantasy of another man when you have the real one standing in front of you. It is an insult to God to push away the one He has prepared for you. He found you, yet still he doesn't measure up to the one in your head.

How dare you push away a man who is working day and night to prove to you that he's a man of integrity to be with a fine dude who doesn't work? Now I am not saying you shouldn't be attracted to him but just because he's fine and everybody wants him does not make him worthy of you. It does not get him out of his grandmother's basement. He may be fine and drive a fancy car, but he still doesn't own anything. He doesn't have a savings or checking account. He gets his checks cashed at the liquor store. But you'd rather have that than the man who's working hard and pulling his credit score up... he has his stuff together. You'd rather have that than to drive around in his smaller car right now. You'd rather choose the dude in the Benz or the BMW even though he lives with his mama... that's right he lives with her she doesn't live with him.

You believed God for a husband and now you're offended when he finds you and gives you something small that he can afford? Because you and your girls are used to watching (un)reality television, with unrealistically big rocks on their hands. You emasculate this good man who is doing his best in this moment. What makes it okay for you to make him think he's not good enough? I have questions. Think about it now. So what if he had to go to Kmart or Walmart to get the best ring he could get? He loves you so much that he chose to be with you and nobody else. And because he loves you, he's didn't want to take out a $5,000 loan to get you a rock. He'd rather put that money aside to save as a down payment on your first house together. So what if he spent $200 on the ring he gave you instead of going into unnecessary debt. This is because he has a plan and vision for you and him. When we have these attitudes, we're teaching our men that size does matter and not their heart. We're teaching them how judgmental and shallow we can be. And it's just not fair.

I say this all the time... as women we have got to get our priorities straight. Do you want the big ring now or do you want the husband with the savings account and goals? He's gonna put some money away for your kids. He's gonna have an insurance policy. He pays his tithes and offerings. He sows. He knows how to respect and love you and his family. He's not gonna leave you home sick with the kids; he's gonna stay home with you. He's not gonna spend more time with the boys than he does with his family. He understands he's a husband first too.

You want a man of God that will cover you, protect you, listen to you, submit to you, and band around you. What does that mean? Look at your ring. Its shape is a circle. Your husband is the band around your family, which is placed in the center of the circle. He bands like a covering around them for safety and protection. He protects you from intruders and intrusion. He fights for you. He doesn't allow harm to come near you. He protects in the spirit and in the natural. The husband that is given to you by God takes that position very seriously. He assures you that no matter what he isn't going anywhere. He places his very existence on the line for his family. And when praying and believing God he is covering his family. Size doesn't matter when you are talking about the husband God has prepared for you. Now let's really talk about size.

Some of you think that if he's not well endowed, he has a problem. I'm here to tell you, he doesn't.

Do you think God was taken by surprise with how He blessed your man? Do you think your man stood in line and asked for an extra small thingy? He didn't pick that. And after all, what is "well endowed" anyway? How many inches does that measure up to be exactly?

The problem is that most of you are coming in to this thing with information you are not supposed to have. You've got some preconceived ideas about what it's supposed to be to be acceptable. And you're holding him accountable for your misinformation. You learned some things fornicating, watching porn, and using dildos and toys. None of which you were supposed to be doing. As a matter of fact, get up right now and go to that secret stash of yours and throw it away! YES, right now! You have him competing with ghosts and objects girl! And now you have the nerve to tell him, he's not big enough to satisfy you.

Let's bottom-line some things here. You think that it is size that's gonna get you "there." Not so much.

Brace yourself for a reality check here. Women need direct clitoral stimulation. You need your husband to put his mouth on you and his fingers on you to get you there most of the time. Size has nothing to do with any of that. By the way, then your marriage bed is undefiled. What happens between you and your husband is blessed by God. Now if you need to use toys due to impotence or maybe you can't have penetration because it can be painful, talk it through and don't be afraid to explore. Be honest with each other. Remember God created sex and desires us to be familiar in the most intimate of ways. It was satan who perverted it. I love how God intended it to be with husband and wife. We become one flesh. I am his and he is mine. I know my husband's body as well as I know my own and he knows mine. For the record, God created sex for husbands and wives, not for "Boohs" and "Baes."

So, ladies, if you made your man feel like he wasn't good enough, you owe him an apology. If you made him feel in any way like he wasn't enough – his money wasn't enough, his education wasn't enough, his car wasn't enough – and he's doing his absolute best, you ought to apologize to him. Lift him up instead of tearing him down. Tell him how much you appreciate him instead of how much you wish he were different.

Start by calling him a Man of God. Just start affirming it. As it is in the spirit realm, so it is in the natural. Start calling him, "Man of God." Tell him how much you appreciate who he is to you and how he treats you. Tell him how much you appreciate his leadership and his being the Head of the Household. That is going to cause such a peace to fall in your house. It's your words that will build him up or tear him down. Watch how God transforms his heart right before your eyes. Begin to pray for him and with him that he is the man God created him to be.

What really happens here is that your eyes and heart are transformed in the process. You stop focusing on everything he's not and begin to see everything he is and always has been. What you focus on, you get more of. How about that? What you focus on, you get more of. The Word of God says, if you keep your mind stayed on Jesus, He'll keep you in perfect peace (Isaiah 26:3). Focus on the peace of the Lord and you have more peace. When your mind is stayed on Jesus, you can't be complaining about what you think your man is lacking, can you? Size doesn't matter. Appreciation and focus do. Now… about this man that I so adore and love.

When he proposed to me it was Christmas Eve going into Christmas day at midnight. Remember I mentioned he and I had been together for a couple of years. I had just had Josiah, which means it was out of wedlock and out of the will of God. I was hurting and rebellious. But Shaun and I worked things out. I promise you… I didn't think that we were gonna get married because of some of the chaos we had been through. But Shaun surprised me. He read me a poem. I sat on his lap and after he finished the poem, he presented me with a ring.

Now, this is not my first marriage, but as I always say it is my perfect marriage. My first marriage was in God's permissive will, not His perfect will. In the first wedding, I had the big dress, the six-foot train, the frilly dress, the $20,000 reception, limos and Corvettes and the big rock. And I paid for that ring dearly with a fool that cheated on me and abused me and left me for days at a time in a city where I knew no one. I really had no business marrying that man. Anyway…

But now, God had reconnected me with my best friend, Shaun, who wound up being the love of my life. And he gave me a band ring. No diamonds, no gems at all. Just silver with gold cuts. And I thought it was the most beautiful ring in the world. And I cried, and I cried, and I cried. I jumped up and down. He asked me to be his wife and will I marry him? Honey, listen, I couldn't wait to marry him. Now, ten years later, I have gone from a band with gold cuts in it to a bridal set to what I wear now, two-and- a-half carats worth of sapphires and diamonds.

I want you to know that God wants big things for you. It might come in stages. It might come after a while. It might come, maybe if later… guess what sis, that's ok.

Don't make that man think he has to take out a second mortgage on your home so you can walk around with a rock right away. Love him where he is and he'll work his butt off to get you this. You want it right. You want it to be blessed. You want to have your priorities straight. You want to be able to grow together and accomplish some stuff together. Pray together, grow together, bond, love hard.

You know what only size should matter? The size of his heart. That matters.

8 DO YOU WANT HIM?

Now if you don't want to forgive him you need to just stop reading this book right now! This is about you right now, not him. Are you ready? Ok Deep BREATHS…1, 2, 3, 4, 5.

I have ministered to wealthy women and middle-class women. Women that are straight up from the hood and at the end of the day they all want the same things security, love, and commitment.

No relationship is perfect no relationship is without flaws… we all have certain battles that we have to fight… we all have insecurities… we all have indiscretions. We all have battled with outsiders and we all have been influenced by negativity too. I won't sit here and pretend that people don't deal with infidelity and cheating emotionally in their relationship hasn't occurred, however that doesn't mean that all is lost.

This doesn't mean that God can't restore… that God can't heal… that God can't replenish… that God can't reconcile if the two agree to work it out and heal and go through the proper wise counsel. Let me say that again… wise counsel… if they forgive and move forward all is not lost.

Now let me be clear about this, if you are the one going through infidelity, emotional or physical abuse and your relationship cannot be saved, please… you need to get the proper help… you need to get the proper information, and tools and the resources to get out of any dangerous emotional and/or physical relationship that will cause you harm and put your life in danger. I just wanna be very clear about that… you do not need to stay in a relationship with someone who is cheating on you recklessly and who is not considering your feelings…

who is not willing to change. If they're not willing to change you need to change your phone number, change your address, change your mind, change the keys to the house, change your change!

When I minister to women who are with men who have cheated or minister to women who are the cheater, a lot of times we get to the root of the matter. A lot of them really did not want to cheat but because they were not yielded and submitted to God according to James 4, they can't resist the devil and have him flee. They ignore the Holy Spirit and make a fleshly decision and they choose to step out of their marriage or step out of their engagement and be involved with someone else.

I've seen people cry and really be remorseful for cheating and it's not that it was something that they planned to do. Sometimes it really did just happen. There's no excuse for it because when you love someone you don't hurt them… when you love someone, you have to not put yourself in a position to cheat. It is a choice. So you can choose to cheat or you can choose not to cheat but when your mind and your spirit are all twisted up in all kind a fleshly desires, resentment and insecurities, hurt and offense, your decision making is altered. Your judgment becomes cloudy so you make dumb decisions.

Women, we must get to the point where we know our husbands and we know them more than they know themselves. We pay attention to the signs, pay attention to what's really going on and not pretending that we don't see. God loves us so much that He always gives us warnings and sometimes the warnings are loud and sometimes there are subtle, they come in a whisper. But we can never say that we had no idea.

Every time a woman tells me that she did not know her husband was cheating, I always ask her are you sure you did not know something, anything? And when I say are you sure you did not know, I don't mean did you not know the details did you not know the woman etc. I mean did you not hear the voice of God? Sis, did you not feel something turning in your spirit in the pit in your belly, did you not see the warning signs? Did you not pay attention? That's what I mean... are you sure you did not know, or did you brush it off as if it was not a big deal?

I saw but I didn't see it. Oh, he didn't mean it that's just his friend. No that's his work buddy. Oh, that's my sister in the Lord or my favorite... they would never do that to me. Ma'am you completely brushed off all the warnings and all the signs that God was trying to show you. Honey, you were not being paranoid or petrified. Listen, you were not that one looking for clues. You were not even looking for a reason for him to cheat. No, it wasn't any of that but when God is trying to show you a thing, don't ignore it! Did we not learn that when someone shows you who you are believe them? I mean the first time according to the late Maya Angelou.

So, my question always leads back to do you want him? Do you want to work things out? Are you able to move on past whatever it is so you can go forth in your marriage? Think about this. The question is do you even want him back? Most of the time when a woman answers this, it's "no I don't want him I don't want nothing to do with him" and I ask them again… are you sure you don't want him back? Because this is the thing, the heart is tender… the heart can be deceitful… the heart can be impressed, and you can see somebody else going through this and think, I'll never go through that or I never want to be the one who was cheated on. Or I'll never forgive him, and he'll never forgive me if I cheated on him and then you exclude God out of the equation… you're making an announcement that you don't believe God can rectify this, you don't believe God can restore, you don't believe God can turn this around and get the glory out of it. You don't believe that if you two come back together that God can heal. So, my question is always again… are you sure? When they consider what I say, most of the time it's I do love him I'm just hurt, and I don't know if I can trust him again. Ok, now we are getting somewhere, that is it! That's the answer I was waiting for.

Be honest, you love him, but you don't know how to trust him again. Now this is where you move out of the way and let God do it. When I say you move out of the way, I mean you move your flesh out of the way. You move your will for revenge out of the way. You move the will to be angry and upset out of the way. You move your selfish desires out of the way. You move opinions of others out the way. You move self-sabotage out of the way and trust God.

Here's the big one, are you ready to put down the spirit of pride for your marriage?

Keep in mind this is not your boyfriend… this is not your booh… this is not somebody you just met the other day… this is your husband. You're covering your soulmate, the one that you made a vow to with God… the one that you said no matter what… You said in sickness and health till death do we part, and he wants to work it out, but do you want to work it out? Are you willing to fight for your marriage? If so, continue reading... if not, skip this chapter now! (Now don't be petty! Read this)

Here are some nuggets and wisdom that I believe will be a real blessing. It's 7 ways to win YOUR man back after cheating and this will work if he wants to change and fight for the relationship/marriage too!

1. Forgive!

This is very important. It's also part of your process. Let it be known that even if you don't want him back you still forgive him and move on with your life. If you decide to stay in the relationship (engagement or marriage) forgive and do not be the person that keeps bringing it back up. What do I mean by that you may ask? If he is making strides to change and is working on rebuilding trust with you, then you are going to have to stop making him pay repeatedly.

2. Learn how to trust him again.

Remember it's a process. If we are learning to trust in the Lord daily, a GOD we don't see, yet we depend on Him, then we have to learn to trust our spouse or significant other again. That takes time, and nobody expects you to trust blindly after being betrayed. Relax, and ask your spouse to be patient with you during this time of building and healing.

3.   Never compare yourself to the other woman.

This is not about her. This isn't about how she looks, her shape, nothing. It was his choice to cross a boundary. You can't beat yourself up and blame yourself. Don't dress like her, do your hair like her, act like her. No way. Now if you want to enhance yourself do it for you but don't you dare compare yourself to her. Again, she is not the problem. He was.

4.   Understand who we are at war with.

The Bible says in the book of Ephesians 6:12 "For we wrestle not against flesh and blood but against principalities, against powers, against the rulers of the darkness of this world, against spiritual wickedness in high places." You're not just dealing with the person but Addiction! Idol worship! Habits! Generational curses! Familiar Spirits! (Deep breath) I know that is a lot, but these must be broken off their life! Praying and fasting comes in here. Put your war clothes on baby girl and WORK!!!! Come against the plans of the devil and tell him "It's on now!" Command every ungodly spirit to leave your marriage, you and your husband.

5.   Listen to what he's really saying.

What does he need help with? You have to know your spouse, does he need more attention, affection, respect etc. You can do this. It's ok to lay down your pride for restoration. What is his "love language"? Focus on that and ask him what he does need. Be open to it, as long as you are not compromising and stepping out of the will of GOD. Remember he is your husband, not your son. Don't tell him how to feel. Don't treat him like a child. Listen to him.

6.   Be honest!

Nobody can answer this question for you but you. Do you want him back? Not the old him but the new him. You have to be real about this. You're going to have to stop being dishonest, if you two can work it out then work it out. No matter what others may say about it.

7.   Stop welcoming their counsel.

Don't allow people who are not wise, people who lack experience, they have no prayer life, they love drama and gossip. Speak into your life! These people are bitter, with way too many failed relationships. They don't respect marriage at all and never point you back to what GOD speaks into your life. Those are the last people you even need to call. Don't reach out to them! When they reach out to you shut it down. It is so important to guard your heart and sit at the feet of people who really want to see you flourish with or without your spouse. Pray and ask God to show you who you can glean and receive from. Remember it should be a safe place and even if they say something or advise you to do something that might stretch you, there should be peace in your heart.

I always felt that cheating is not just about sex, but the emotional affairs are just as bad, if not worse. I can list off a few like social media affairs, sending videos and pictures via text or email. Engaging in pornography and perverted daydreaming. If you want to be free, get free for real from it all! When I have one on ones or teach my classes, I hit on this topic very hard because people think that the actual act of sex is the problem. But what about the things that lead up to it. What about the things I mentioned? These can be deal breakers for sure and isn't it amazing how people don't view it as bondage or cheating too. I remember how my ex-husband would turn on porn while we would engage in the act of sex. I knew it was wrong, I never felt right about it. It opened a door where I started watching it and living in this fantasy world too. Comparing the men I watched, to him. He would have me try things and I would want him to try things with me. It was perverse and wrong. It took me being honest that I had an addiction to porn and ask GOD to take the desire away from me. Well that also meant me throwing away DVDs, VHS tapes, and wiping out my cookies on the internet. I was serious about my deliverance. He continued, but I had to do what was best for me. I was responsible for me not him. Yes, I did pray for him and even tried to throw things away, but he wasn't having it. When it was all said and done he always chose him and I had to be ok with choosing me.

Bonus

Free yourself from withholding sex from your spouse. It's important to come together and make love. Don't let days and weeks go by without intimacy. That can also open up another door for the enemy to creep in and cause havoc. Stay on top of that LITERALLY!

Story time!

There was a couple that was in TROUBLE honey, I mean big time. I gave the wife advice and told her to be open to try new things. She had to say, "Well to prove my point I don't give him sex." Well you know what I said. THAT IS STUPID! Why would you do something like that. Don't keep yourself from him. Shut that mess down. Well she did what I told her, and he said anytime I am hosting an event or class he's sending her. They are thriving and doing very well right now. I praise GOD for that. Sis enjoy your husband and as often as you can. You need sex just like he does. Sex is his way of expressing himself to you. Don't take that from him and punish him. That is wrong and it's not of GOD. Oh, do you want to know what it is? I am going to tell you anyway.

- Control
- Manipulation
- Witchcraft
- Mean
- Unfair

So, change your mind… as a matter of fact go take a break real quick. The book isn't going anywhere.

9 THEY ARE STILL IN YOU

Let's open this up with prayer.

Father, in the name of Jesus, before we ask for a thing we want to just thank you. Thank you for loving us. Thank you for showing us where we are. Thank you for being a hiding place. You didn't uncover us when you could have. You show us how merciful you are, and grace follows us daily. We don't take this moment for granted. I prophesy now that the reader is going to be pulled and snatched out of the clutches of the enemy even now. I speak full freedom over the life of the reader! We thank you in advance for deliverance. There will be no hindrance, setbacks, strongholds or illegal attachments. Nothing binding and pulling them to their past. Father I praise and thank you for the indwelling and the power of the

Holy Spirit. I speak chains be broken, burdens lifted, and yokes destroyed now in the name of Jesus. I believe it to be done. Amen.

Brace yourself, this chapter is longer than the others. I hope you are ready for this will be a time of breakthrough! I get so excited when I think about what this is going to mean for you. Begin to decree and declare breakthrough even before you see or experience it. Begin to get your spirit of expectation up. It's your time. Know this: I was a whole mess! SERIOUSLY if He can do it for me, He can most certainly do the same or better for you. I am going to stand in agreement with heaven for you and believe God for the best to come in your life. That you will see manifestation quickly! I feel Him as I write this and prepare for this time together. I can literally feel the presence of God. I feel like I could run! (I won't, but I would!)

We're going to uncover the real marriages some of you are engaged in and have been for a long time. You may have never thought about it in this way before, but this will bless you at least it's my hope that it blesses you as much as it blessed me.

Here we are and the question is: who are you married to? Are they still in there? I know some of you are saying, "Markita, I'm married to my husband." And some others of you are saying, "I'm not married at all yet." Well, I'm here to tell you that some of you are illegally married in the spirit. That means that you have ungodly attachments, or what we hear often in the church the phrase "soul ties" to people that you are not married to in the natural. You have spiritual attachments to people from your past that are ungodly. Some of you are so stuck in your past that you can't even embrace your now. Some of you want to be married and want to be a "Good Thang". The reason you haven't been able to do that is because you are so used to doing it in the ungodly way, you have been outside of the will of God. They are still in you! Many of you are still married to your past. Your mind and heart longs to be elsewhere and you don't know why.

About 2 years ago, God gave me a great revelation on how some of his daughters are still very much married and attached to prior relationships. He said to me you are married in the spirit and married through connections, sexual and non-sexual. Some connections are emotional and mental. Others were just verbal contracts. We have made vows to people that we should never have made vows to. We made promises that God never intended for us to make to people we should not have been making promises to. Oh, and by the way, this applies to friendships, social media, business relationships, and church as well!

The problem is that you've never repented and denounced those promises and never broken them. You've pretended to get over it and try to move on… my dear, they still exist in your spirit. You never asked God to forgive you, you have never forgiven yourself. You never asked God to deliver you from it. You never said, "God I was out of your will. I was not doing things within your perfect will. I

was in the permissive realm or being very emotional.
I was being very naive to the devices of the enemy. I
made stupid and silly decisions and therefore made a
covenant a vow with someone I should never have
been in covenant with."

We all have made connections to people that we
should never have had any connection to. Every last
one of us has said, "I got you. If no one else got
you... I got you." We all have done it. It comes
completely from our flesh and God's permissive will.
We have all promised, "I'm never going to leave you,
babe. No matter what. No matter what, you'll always
be mine." We've all said something similar to this. I
myself suffered too long because I made vows to
people and they weren't sexual but they were
perverted because it wasn't the plan of the Lord for
my life! I did that. Because I'm loyal. And it meant
something to me to be that kind of loyal. So if I'm
with you, I'm with you. And you will probably have
to break up with me before I break up with you

because I'm just that type of woman. If I was with somebody, I was with somebody.

Then, reality set in! I went through abandonment, rejection and then came rebellion. I was just totally outside of God's will. I was bouncing around from man to man, friend to friend. And then I got in real trouble because I was always angry. I was depressed. I wasn't suicidal, but I easily could have been because I had all this stuff in me. All of these men's spirits were in me, all of these fake friends connected to me. Their words were in me. In some cases, these men's fluids were in me. Ugh! I would wake up one day just angry because I slept with someone that had anger issues. I would wake up... sometimes feeling really, really confused and depressed because the body I dealt with was bi-polar and I didn't know it! THIS STUFF IS REAL!!!! You ever been around somebody you dated and started acting like them and wondered why? How about this? You watched a certain TV show and began to really think that was your life? We have to be careful about what we attach ourselves to.

I had a conversation with a young lady and I said to her "Listen to me… no matter where or when you move, this person will always have a piece of your heart, if you don't get him out your spirit." She told me that she didn't know how to let go even though he moved on with his life and has another family and doesn't speak to her. This is what I am saying, We spoke that foolishness into our lives. We get caught up saying, "No matter who you're with, you'll always be my man. No matter where you go, you'll always be my friend, my bro or sis. No matter what I'll never leave this church, this alliance, this organization etc." And then we wonder why we can never get over an individual or people.

Have you ever seen a picture and instantly have a flash back? Or we have a memory and we stay and think about yesteryear. That's a problem and we reminisce too long then we feel those same feelings all over again. I need you to know that person or those people are still inside of you! I want to let you know that God wants you to be completely free. He wants us to be completely free, not somewhat free, not a little bit free. Free from it all.

He needs you to see that...

1. It is a trick of the enemy. Understand that right now. He wants to sabotage you. Destroy you and it starts with what you're still attached to.

2. You think you have the strength and courage to move on from it on your own and you don't. This has to be dealt with face to face, severed, dismantled and broken! Some people think even fasting is old school and extreme, but honey, it WORKS!

3. That it is a device to try to keep you bound. It makes you say, "I'm over it," and you're really not. Honesty is the name of game. Tell the truth.

I love that I am free from these things, so I can freely talk about them with you. I promise that you are not alone. I know what it feels like to be all over the place physically and mentally and, at the end the day, it still all felt just nasty. I would wake up sometimes just really, really sad because somebody I was dealing with was always on an emotional rollercoaster. I laid down with these demons... willingly and sometimes the strongman took over and I wasn't in control at all, that spirit tempting me was because I wasn't yielded or submitted to GOD. Intentionally and Unintentionally I did that.

It wasn't until I had my very own "one-on-one" with the Lord and I said, "God what is this?, why can't I shake this? I keep thinking about him! I can't seem to forgive this one and that one. I am trying to move forward! I sing, I worship, I quote scripture after scripture. Why can't I break free?" He said, "You made a covenant with people. You made a vow to them without asking me. When you became one with them you made covenant with them." And that is Truth. They are still in there! We became one with unholy connections, whether it's the will of God or not for our lives. We came into agreement with them. And so now you have opened yourself up to receive whatever is in that person. You agree with their stuff at a cellular level. That's deep... I know.

You embraced and accepted their stuff as your own. I have to say it again. Some of you have made verbal connections and verbal vows to people with whom you had no business doing that.

Now let me talk about marriage again. In my course, the Wifely Way, we teach you that God is preparing us for marriage. We want our husbands to find us being who we are in God. Except they can't find us because we have made a connection and come into agreement with another man. It's like having a force field around you, making that one who is trying to find you, unable to see you. It's like you're invisible to him, he's really looking but doesn't know where to start. And no matter how much you want to protest and disagree that you are married to the other man, it doesn't change the fact that according to heaven you are. In the spirit you are. You've got to take ownership of that. It is the only way to be delivered and healed from your past.

This might be hard to address but I have to go here too. Some of us have been molested. Some of us have been raped. Some of us have been abused. We've been in and out of relationships trying to fit in. We want them to love us and want them to be there. Then… when they don't work out, we blame them, because we say in our mind, we did everything right. In actuality, we did not. We did not do everything right.

Bonus, I am a certified life coach, a licensed minister, and more, but if you need to see a counselor besides Jesus and your best friend, please get the help you need and don't be afraid or ashamed to talk it through. Pretending it didn't happen will never make it go away. It wasn't until I talked about how my Godbrother tried to rape me that I was able to forgive him for real and not hold on to anger anymore. It wasn't until I was able to talk about my divorce that I was able to put things in the proper perspective. GET HELP if you need it. If you don't it will spill out in other areas of your life.

There are times we will have to deal with the consequences of our actions, it's just life. And I'm not saying we're playing victim and asking for a darn pity party either. What I am saying is that we've got to be accountable for the things that we did agree to. We are accountable for some of the hurt, the pain, the frustration, the shame and the humiliation that came when we chose to be intertwined with these people. We made that decision out of our flesh, apart from the will of God. And that's what we should never have done.

So now we have to ask God to help us and to realign us and prepare us for a "divorce". I know, you're saying, God doesn't like divorce. No, he does not like divorce but that doesn't change the fact that these marriages that He also doesn't like… have to end. What's in you has to come out!

So… we ask God now to prepare us for the separation.

Help us with the annulment.

I'm going to bring you to the Word of God about knitting souls together and soul ties and things of that nature. First Samuel 18:1: "As soon as he had finished speaking to Saul, the soul of Jonathan was knit to the soul of David, and Jonathan loved him as his own soul." That is an example of knitting a soul together or the intertwining of souls together, in other words there was an instant bond between David and Jonathan. They became covenant brothers. They weren't blood brothers but they became covenant brothers and so they made a vow to each other. That is an example of a bond or godly attachment. They made a covenant vow to each other. All soul knitting (bonding) or connections are not perverse. They're not sexual. That is important to know. You can have a heart connection without having a sexual relationship. It's about the emotional and mental connection between people.

Here's another example of a spirit connection. Let's look at Hebrews 4:12: "For the Word of God is living and active, sharper than any two-edged sword piercing to the division of the soul and of the spirit of joint and of marrow and discerning thoughts and intentions of the heart." This is all spirit connection. Now here is an example of the immoral soul tie. 1 Corinthians 6:18: "Flee from sexual immortality. Every other sin a person commits outside the body, but the sexual immoral person sins against his own body." This is especially for the wives. Genesis 2:24: "Therefore a man shall leave his father and mother and hold fast or cleave to his own wife and they shall become one flesh." Pay attention to this: Genesis 2:24: "And therefore a man shall leave his father and his mother and hold fast or cleave to his own wife and they shall become one flesh." Here again is the husband and wife coming together.

The highest form of worship between a husband and a wife is not them lifting their hands in worship. You know, speaking in tongues and praising and dancing and falling out. The highest form of worship for husband and wife, the highest works of the husband and wife, is when they come together in sexual intercourse and love making. Shut ya mouth, say what? Yes, I said it. That's why it is important that you do not open yourself up to being with just anybody. I really need you to hear me on this. I want you to hear my heart when I say it is not okay to test the waters! It's not ok to test drive the car. It's not ok to taste and see if it's good before marriage! (Lord have mercy, you laughing right, huh?). It's not OK to do things the way the world does, as much as the church tries to fit into the world's ways. It's not OK for you to try to see if he's big enough; if he can take you there. It's not OK for you to give your body to somebody that it doesn't belong to because when you marry you start thinking about your exes. Trust me on this. I'm not telling you something I heard about or that someone told me. I'm telling you the truth I've lived through. When I got married, I had to fight the images of my exes. I had to fight the thoughts of where I used to be with other men while I was married.

I had to ask God, "I love my husband. I'm in love with my husband. My husband gets me there. He takes good care of me. Heck! My husband rock's my boat. He makes me feel all kinds of good inside. I mean like a NATURAL woman, ok? Why has that image come back? I don't want that." God said, "that spirit is still in you." That really kind of blew me away! I couldn't imagine that person was still with me. I asked God, "What do you mean that spirit is still in me?" He said, "You did not call their name out. You did not cut the ties and attachments. You did not denounce it. You did not break it. You did not sever it. You did not come against it. That means that person is still in you." You may not even remember their name. But because you didn't ask God to deliver you, they're still inside of you. Some people don't believe in that. There are some people that are just dumb enough to believe that spiritual deposits are not real.

Spirits transfer. That is truth.
Some of you are walking around angry at your husband, blaming him for what somebody did to you two or three years ago, ten years ago, twenty years ago. And you don't understand why it makes

you mad when your husband does a certain thing. It makes you mad because homeboy did that and you forgot about it.

You forgot about it, but your spirit didn't forget. Your flesh forgot about it, your intellect forgot about it, your conscious forgot about it but your subconscious didn't! Wow, it just got real again! It's still back there thinking, "Why don't I like it when you wear that? I picked it out." What you don't remember is that you picked it out for somebody else and when you got mad at that person you didn't like that outfit anymore.

That is why it is important before you get married to be honest with yourself. To be honest with God and say, "God anything in me, even the things I don't remember... If it's not of you, if there's not a Godly connection, if it's not ordained, not healthy, then get it out of me."

I had another "one-on-one" with the Lord. I had a conversation with God and I began to write down names and call out to God. And I began to cry, damn that list was long. See some of you can't be free cause you won't be honest, but I am free! I slept with this person. I touched this person. I stayed on the phone too long with this person. I had a mental connection with this person and I gave too much information about me to this person. I let that person see too much. I was naked in front of this person. I let this person cross a boundary with me. I let this person in too much. I made a covenant vow with this person. I started to weep harder, "God take them out of me, take it away, I don't want them and what comes with them! I release it all to you!" I actually counted the names. And then there were some people I forgot about. I told God "whatever it takes, whatever it is, I don't want to bring this into my Now.

I don't want to bring this into my now situation. I don't want to bring this to my current situation. This is not fair to my husband."

The Bible says while we're on this earth our days are full of trouble; I don't want to add to that. I want to enjoy my husband. And for you single ladies: you want to enjoy your life while you're single. You can still date. You can still enjoy yourself. You could still go out and have a good old time. But when you start adding sex and impure thoughts or when you're having perverted conversation you are entering dangerous territory. And some of you are saying, "I don't fornicate. I don't have sex." But you are having impure thoughts, impure conversation. Some of you are even engaging in self-gratification, that's right! Masturbation when you're single is unholy girl. I told you early in this book, throw it or them things away! I know the world says it's healthy touching yourself and pleasing yourself but that's out of God's will. It's perversion. What are you thinking about? You have to be honest with yourself to be free from it. It's a trap to keep you from your full potential to be a good wife.

A good wife is not a woman that sits in the corner and is quiet. A good wife is not a woman who just sits around waiting for her husband to tell her what to do. She does not kowtow to her husband. Even though I have no problem doing whatever he likes, that's not all there is to me and that is not all there is to you.

"Yes. Whatever you want. Whatever you want, dear." No! You are not a sex slave either (Now if you want to role play in your house with your husband knock yourself out!). You want to bring all that you are to your husband. Everything that God had placed in you before he came is what you want to bring into the marriage. You don't lose your voice just because you get married. You are still you... bringing all of who you are enhances the joining together of the two of you. And to you single women, you want to be sure of who you are and certain that you know who you are. Throughout the chapters so far, we dealt with who you are. And we dealt with knowing who God said you are. If you knew who you were, if you really knew who you were, you wouldn't just let everybody fool with you and waste your time. You don't have time to waste.

You also wouldn't let people talk to you any kind of way. You wouldn't compromise so much. You wouldn't fall for the trick. You would have so much self-respect and value that no one could take that place with you except your husband.

If you really knew who you were you wouldn't put limitations on yourself. So we learned that we don't have to be the side-chick. We learned that we are not a "wifey" but a wife and not just a wife, but a good wife. Do you know who you are? Do you know that God calls you Favored? Do you know that you are a treasure? And until he finds you, you should remain hidden. Hidden doesn't mean that you are buried so deep that no one can find you, but it certainly means that not everybody should have access to you. You've got to know your value. Everybody can't touch you.

Everybody can't converse with you. And that is not you being stuck-up. You are guarding yourself and using wisdom this time because you don't want to come into contact with things that are not of

God. You do not want to come into covenant with things and people and spirits that are not healthy, that are not of God. That would be to your detriment. Hear me well on this. It would be to your detriment. I never understood why I would see young ladies having babies with guys who had 30 babies already. And she is really thinking that if she has his baby he won't treat her the same way. I do not understand what she is thinking!

Then the Lord showed me that every woman he slept with she slept with too. Doesn't that just make ya mad? Every woman he deposited into, he grabbed to their spirit and she grabbed to his. So, when he lay down with another woman, the same thing happened over again. He grabbed her spirit and she grabbed his. And it was a ripple effect that just kept going with each new person. So, all the women thought the same thing. All the women said the same thing: "He won't do that to me. I'm different. He really loves me. He even said so. I can take care of his kids. I'm not like those others he left.

I can change him. He just needs somebody to understand him." Now we're talking ten, fifteen kids later, he's still sleeping around. He's got a new woman saying, "He won't do that to me." You've adopted that spirit. You've taken that so-called "truth" and made your own story. And now it has manifested in you. I ask women all the time, "Why would you stay with someone that's hitting you?" They all say, "Because he loves me." I ask, "Why do you believe that?" "Because my mom used to get hit and my dad loved her." So that's the explanation? Here we go again with cycles and patterns that are not of GOD. These are things that you really believe and have come into agreement with and made true for you. You have come into agreement with things that are not holy. Then you wonder why you go through what you go through.

You've got to be able to hear this truth. You have got to be able to accept the truth for what it is and apply it to your life. You cannot be afraid to face the real facts and take responsibility for it, be accountable for it. You have the chance to get it right today, right now. It is not God's will for your life to just be pulled under and suffocated. It's not His will for you. Don't forget sis… You have the chance right now to start over, start fresh. You've got to forgive. You've got to denounce these people. You've got to let the ungodly relationships go in order for you to be the greatest wife you could ever be. Because being a great wife has nothing to do with just being pretty and having sex and being silent. Being a bad wife is not just about opening up your mouth and being disrespectful and rolling your neck and not cooking and cleaning. Some of you are bad wives because you don't tell your husband the truth. At the right time, you have to tell him "thus says the Lord" whether he likes it or not. You hear GOD too! Some of you are bad wives because you don't hold your husband accountable to the vision. Some of you are bad wives because you won't pray for your husband.

I'M STILL OLD FASHIONED!

The term "soul tie" is not used in the Bible, but again I understand why it's being said amongst the church, remember it's the bond (knitting of souls) it's the spiritual attachment. For married couples, it is an almost magnetic pull between them that draws them together.

Spiritual attachments that develop between fornicators is dangerous and it can draw a beaten and abused woman to an abusing partner. He treats her like trash and doesn't love her. Even so, she turns to him for validation and regard that she will never receive. It's demonic.

How are these attachments formed?
These are some of the ways I know of that addiction, idolatry and ungodly attachments are formed:

A couple of ways are through sexual relations and emotional attachments. However, Godly bonds or soul knitting are formed between a married couple according to Ephesians 5:31, "For this cause shall a man leave his father and mother and shall be joined or cleave to his wife. And the two shall become one flesh." And a godly bond between a husband and wife as God intended is for it to be unbreakable. You can also have these bonds with your children, friends, family members etc.

However, when a person has ungodly relationships with other people, that ungodly is formed. "What know ye not which ye have joined to a harlot? Now as one body." Do you know what a harlot is? Harlot is whore, slut, or nasty girl. Freak. Trick. This connection fragments the soul and is destructive. People who have many past relationships find it very difficult to bond or be joined to anybody because their heart and spirit is fragmented.

Close relationships is another way godly attachments are formed. I want to remind you about Ruth and Naomi, as well as King David and Jonathan had good godly attachments as a result of good friendship and loyalty. Ruth left her land and followed Naomi, her mother-in-law, who she honored and loved. Wherever she went, Ruth was down with her… no matter what! With David and Jonathan "So it came to pass that when he made an end of speaking unto Saul that the soul of Jonathan was knit unto the soul of David. And Jonathan loved him as his own soul."

Bad soul knitting can come from bad relationships as well. Idolizing someone can form an ungodly attachment. Conversation can cause an ungodly attachment. Imagine that you know somebody is trifling, or out of order. You know someone is ignorant. You know someone is foolish. You know someone is mean, manipulative, demonic, and you still commit to them, telling them, "No matter what, I got you." but you now have committed idolatry to that person and have a strong addiction to them.

How do you break a spiritual attachment? You break it by denouncing that person. You break an attachment by asking God to sever, break and deliver. You repent for submitting your body a living sacrifice to them and not the Lord. Every time you ask God to get them out of you, He does it. He moves. It happens quickly. He does it because He knows you're serious about being in right relationship with Him and about breaking the ties you created through your flesh.

This is why God wants us to present our bodies as a living sacrifice, holy unto Him and acceptable. This is why they that worship Him must worship Him in spirit and in truth. Not in some truth, not in part of a truth, not in lies. Not in tipping around, always repenting. You repent every day about the same thing but never change. You're not delivered. You need to be delivered. My mother used to say, "I smell sin on you," and just look at me and walk away. No matter how many times I would take a shower. No matter how many times I soaked. No matter how many times I sprayed perfume. Or tried to scrub that stuff off, she would still sniff around me, smellin' sin on me. How did she know? That's how God looks at us. Every time we fall.

I'M STILL OLD FASHIONED!

Get up woman and Stop falling! Don't open up the door to sin, fall into sin, get up, dust yourself off and start walking again, only to fall in again. Stop falling, hold on to God so you can be the best wife you can be!

Now pay attention… not everyone will be married! And shame on wives who look down on women who are not married. Truth be told, some of us should not have gotten married when we did. So stop that too! I minister to single women who do not want marriage yet still want to enjoy their lives. You can do that and still not practice sexual sin. There are still some women out there that are pure and not fornicating. Know that.

So here is how to break spiritual attachments:

1.   Worship – that is the strongest thing you could ever do. You must get into the spirit to worship.

2.   Repentance – "God forgive me." You've got to ask with sincerity and seriousness. Not

with the intention to do the same thing all over again.

3.   Denounce the person – Ask God to cleanse you of that person's spirit, flesh, and essence.

4.   Fast and Pray- Matthew 17:21. But this kind does not come out only by prayer and fasting.

You may not remember who they are. Or don't remember what they looked like. You don't remember where you were. But you remember the scent. You remember the moment. Your flesh and the devil want you to remember the feeling.

Before I was free, I remembered ten years ago, nine years ago, a couple of months ago, last week, I remember that. And I don't like how that makes me feel on the inside. "Whatever that is, God you know what it is. Get it out of me. Take it out of my memory! Create in me a clean heart and renew a right spirit within me. Cast me not away from your presence." A sinner cannot be in the presence of God. A sinner can be in the presence of Jesus, but not in the presence of God. Even in the Old

Testament, when the priests had to go behind the veil, they had to wear bells at the bottom of their garment. If there was any sin on them at all, they would drop dead in the presence of God.

We're talking about the priests that were in the synagogue, in the temple. Any sin on them, they would immediately drop dead. They would be dragged out from behind the veil by a rope wrapped around their waist.

When the burning bush was flaming, God said to Moses, "Take off your sandals. This is holy ground. You can't bring that stuff before Me. I am God."

So, we must repent of doing ungodly things. You must ask God to forgive you for making these connections to people. Forgive you for decisions you made because you felt badly in your heart for them. Nobody else wanted to be their friend. And you wanted to be their friend. They didn't have anybody else. And now we must ask God to break it.

I'm not talking about breaking chains here. This is a spirit and spirits are not chains. A chain can come back together. You know that if you've ever had a necklace and it came apart. You got some pliers and pulled the link apart to hook it back together. We're not talking about chains here. We're talking about spirits breaking off my life. God, snatch it out of me. I don't want that anymore because I want to be a great wife. I want to submit to my husband.

It was hard for me to submit to my husband because the last man that I was with made me feel less than, like I was a slave. Or like I was beneath him. The last person that I was with made me feel insignificant. They made me feel like I wasn't an achiever. It crushed me. Now that I'm married to this person, I always fight. I'm always trying to prove who I am. Because I really wanted to fight the person that made me feel this way! But I didn't have enough strength to fight that person. So, before I let you come up on me, I'm gonna fight you first. I'm gonna swing first. I already know what you're gonna say, so before I let you get one more word out, I'm gonna attack. Even though that person has not come to fight. This is a set up from the enemy to have you all messed up in the head. It's time to let go of what came before and the expectation of a fight.

Be honest now. You talk to your husband crazy don't you? You put your husband through hell. And he's not going to tell you because every time he tries to tell you, he hears you on the phone dragging him through some more with your friends and family. So, since he can't tell you, I will. Hush! Watch how you talk to him. Some of you are just downright mean! Remember... listen to what he is really saying. You would never talk to the person who made you feel that way in the first place this way. So why are you doing it to the one that loves you the most? We're talking about doing things the Wifely Way.

We want to get completely free from our past, so we can embrace and enjoy where we are. And enjoy being married! I'm going to challenge some of you wives to go to your husbands tonight and apologize. And apologize sweetly. "Baby, I'm sorry. I've been talking to you all kinds of crazy." Now he's probably going to think that you are trying to kill him. So, don't ask him about the insurance policy tonight. He's probably going to look at you like, "What did you put in the food?" Just assure him that you're not trying to kill him. Be sincere and tell him again that you apologize for talking to him crazy. Then tell him that you know you weren't over some things. You don't have to go into detail. He already knows you're nuts and he loves you anyway. Just tell him that there are some areas where you thought you were healed and you really weren't. And you took it out on him and you're really sorry. And give him a hug and kiss. Some of you can do a little bit more. And build from there. Appreciate that man and let him know you're gonna get this thing right. And be excited about it. Then start doing things the Wifely Way. Stop withholding from your husband. Stop putting him on punishment. That is foolish and stupid.

I'M STILL OLD FASHIONED!

If you are single, be ok with being ALONE! You are not lonely. Loneliness means being sad, unhappy and socially isolated. No, you might be alone but you're not about to embrace depression through loneliness. If you're single, there is no reason you don't have a passport. You need to be travelling outside of your city, region and state. If you are single, you need to start doing things outside of your neighborhood. You are so good at saying there are no good men out there. Of course, there are. They are just outside of your area. You may have to go where they are. Even when you are dating online, you can develop an attachment with somebody... watch that! You're lusting after people you don't even know! They are ghosts. That may not even be his real picture. You may not be fornicating, but you are on there, flirting, sending pictures and talking nasty. You are still intertwining with these people. That's developing an ungodly spiritual attachment. You have to break the ungodly connections so that God can send you the right man.

I would be willing to bet that you have, at some time in your life, created a list of qualities that you want in your husband. Am I right? Be honest. And most of the stuff on your list was shallow and petty. You wanted someone tall, dark and handsome. He had to have swag like Denzel or Idris. He had to be Drake and Trey Songz for the youngins. He had to have just the right smile and the right build like Dwayne "The Rock" Johnson. He had to make you laugh like Kevin Hart and Marlon Waynes. He had to smell right and sound right with a deep, sexy voice that would whisper the right words in your ear. Okay, dream time is over. Wake up princess! He's probably not gonna have all of that, I can pretty much guarantee it. You left off the most important aspects of your husband. You need to start the list with how much he loves God and loves you the way God created him to love you. Add that he prays with and for you daily. Add that he is considerate and kind and thoughtful. Add that his character is strong and solid. Add that he respects and admires you.

Add that he is highly regarded in the community and at his workplace. Add that he has a generous heart. Now you've started a list that has meat and promise. All that other stuff is nice, but it is not lasting. It is not the stuff upon which a strong marriage is built.

10 THE GOOD THANG!

Well so far so good! It got very real and intense that last chapter. Get you a glass of water or something stronger (Ginger ale of course)! Within these pages, we've been talking about how women every day are destroying themselves trying to get married at best, or trying to just have a man, any man, at worst. Well I am here to tell you and your friend that you're sharing this book with, that's just simply not ok to do anymore. No, baby girl, you will no longer settle.

I think about all the queens and sisters I've seen demean themselves and the God in them by not just wearing revealing clothes, now folks like to be butt naked, going to bars and clubs trying to be picked, selected, chosen.

The term that I hate but comes to mind "Thirsty" in the urban dictionary it means:

1. Too eager to get something.

2. Desperate.

I don't know about you but the only one I want to be

"desperate" for is the LORD! I do understand the pain and desperation of some people; brokenness and loneliness compel them into worldly ways of finding a partner hoping for a spouse and companion. This leads to more heartache and despair. Sunday (or Saturday for the 7th day Adventist readers) morning, they stand ashamed before God. The Holy Spirit convicts them in God's presence. We talked about how sin cannot dwell in the presence of God's perfect holiness. We praise Him for the gift of repentance, though we should not be repenting for the same thing repeatedly. You must change your mind and not do it again. That's true repentance. Would you trust and believe somebody that kept doing the same thing with no change at all? Think about that.

I know it's hard. I've been there. I have lived it but what I know and can stand on is that there can be joy in the waiting. I'll say that one more time. There is joy in the waiting!!! Let's be honest… do you really want the one you found in the bar, you know the one that just bought you drinks and maybe danced with you? Meanwhile he's buying drinks for her, her and maybe him too! What makes you think he'll marry, honor and respect you when you looked like a harlot when he met you? You remember what a harlot is, right? And now that you got his attention, you want to dress conservatively and go to church with him. Not. He still wants to see you twerking dropping it low and sipping! He doesn't want to see you for Jesus either! Lol.

Now this will set some of you struggling here free! Are Christians supposed to find their spouse in the bar? Are they supposed to find them in the church? I will say this: just because he goes to church or serves in church doesn't mean he's, saved, delivered, or that he is your husband. Stop thinking you're going to change him into the Godly King your heart wants him to be. And be real, if you are following God and devoted to serving Him with your life, then marrying a non-believer is not even close to being an option unless there are boundaries set about your individual belief systems, and I don't recommend it. You must be careful mixing different belief systems. By the way, I am not only referring to the unsaved woman. Some saved women just wear me out. Hiding behind church all the while just as confused and grasping at straws too. Saved but have no self-awareness. Saved but have no confidence. Saved and have no prayer life at all. I have seen religious women settle and I wanted to just grab them and say, "Get out of this! This isn't God's best." As a matter of fact, I have grabbed women and would shake them! I knew a woman very close to me and she was married for many years to a man who she felt "loved" her. He played so many emotional games with her. He tormented her.

Don't let that be you. Don't trick yourself into thinking "staying" with someone who isn't willing to change means you're in the will of the Lord either.

A popular marriage scripture is Proverbs 18:22: "Whoso findeth a wife findeth a good thing and obtaineth favor from the Lord." Based on this scripture, women have repeatedly been admonished to "be the good thing he finds." Be the wife. That's what we've been talking about in this work.

It is proven science that men benefit from marriage.

The Proverbs 18:22 passage refers to the institution of marriage being the good thing he finds. It didn't say, "When he finds a lady." It didn't say, "When he finds a partner." It didn't say, "When he finds a girlfriend, a lover, a mistress." It specifically states that he who finds a "wife" finds a good thing and obtains favor from the Lord. As his wife, you are part of the favor he finds. Favor means

APPROVED! GOOD! How you doing GOOD
THANG?!

I want to say this though make sure that he is
your husband. You're the good "thang" right? Well
he should be ready and worthy to have you. You
can't be ready, and he is not. Women ask me all the
time, "How did you know Shaun was the one?" It's
such an easy, yet hard, question for me to answer.
The best answer I can give is that I really liked Shaun
as a person before I loved him. He was my friend. I
knew Shaun was the one when I couldn't go a day
without talking to him. Because I enjoyed his
company. I knew he was the one when he stood up
for me and didn't apologize for loving me. I knew
Shaun was the one when he developed his own
relationship with God and was sincere. I knew he
was the one when he chose me through it all. So,
don't marry someone you lust for but don't like and
love. Don't marry if you're clearly unsure he will
choose you through it all!

I'M STILL OLD FASHIONED!

Well ladies, we've covered a lot of ground in this work so far. And now we need to apply what we've learned. Application is very important. You can't just read this and walk it out. After all, we're in this to make life look and be different, more like what brings us joy in the Lord and in the home. What is the point if nothing in your life changes or you still don't feel like you have what you need to have the manifest blessings of the Lord?

We talked a little bit about the extraordinary qualities of the Virtuous Woman and the responsibilities of a wife. A huge part of that responsibility is to be someone he wants to find. So now we know that you're a woman but are you a wife wanting to be found? I can hear you saying

"Yessssssss" but hold up. Think about this now. Are you ready? This is not to scare you and turn your heart from marriage at all. You just have to be sure.

Ok so we talked about being the hidden treasure.

Hidden treasure is worth finding. Work on becoming the woman a godly Christian man would want to find... and marry... NO SETTLING! Of course, that starts with the desire to be a godly wife.

This is serious. The Word of God says, "Seek ye ... the kingdom of God and His righteousness, and all these things shall be added unto you" (Matthew 6:33). The added unto you includes the godly husband. But look at what it says first. It's not enough to want to be a godly wife to have the husband. The desire to please and know God intimately must come first and it must stand alone. Remember, we said that in your marriage God comes first for both of you? That starts here. You must first desire a relationship with God, seeking Him, loving Him, wanting more of Him, and desiring to please Him before the godly husband will come. This is also related to knowing who you are.

Ask God in this process to show you to you as He sees and knows you. It will blow your mind! When sometimes all we can see is all that's wrong,

He sees us through His perfection in us. He says that when we repent and ask forgiveness of our sins, He throws them as far away from us as the east is from the west (Psalm 103:12). He throws them into the depths of the sea (Micah 7:19) where they exist no more. We focus on our mistakes. He sees only His forgiveness. We focus on everything we got wrong and bring that stuff up. He sees only how much He loves us. He sees the blood of Jesus. Be still and know that He is God and His mercy is enough to cover all of your wrongs when you repent and forgive yourself. I challenge you to spend some of your private time with Him asking Him to show you how He regards you. Then embrace that Truth as your own. I challenge you to write things down in a journal, get it all out and then THROW it away! I challenge you to look at yourself in the mirror and speak four great things about what you're believing God to do in your personal life. I want you to rid yourself of every negative thought you've had about yourself and not look back.

Are you ready? Here's the plan… to become the godly wife that is the found treasure. Create the person of "wife" now and the godly man will be presented to you. I'm not talking about "acting as if" or faking it 'til you make it mess… that's fake and people see through that. I mean you should become the wife that you want to be with the qualities and characteristics she would have. No more "Faking IT", it's about "Being IT".

Think about this now, would a "Good Thang" go clubbing on the regular? Would a "Good Thang" eat out every day? Would a "Good Thang" publicly wear revealing clothes to entice other men? Would a "Good thang" lie, cheat, manipulate and argue? Would a "Good Thang" not keep her word? Would a "Good thang" put others before her husband? Would a "Good thang" not cover her husband and family too? Would a "Good Thang" be suspicious of her husband and not trust him? Would a "Good Thang" cause harm to her husband? I'm talking about the "GOOD THANG" now. This isn't for folk playing house. This isn't "Play Skool".

Would a godly wife or good thang cause strife in her household? Would a "good thang" skip prayer and time with the Lord to be on the phone gossiping, causing discord and dragging other people and right in front of her husband? Would a "good thang" allow her home to be cluttered and disorganized? Would a "good thang" allow the laundry to pile up? Would a "good thang" talk about her husband's faults with her friends? This is getting good! Would a "good thang" disrespect her marriage vows? Would a "good thang" expect her husband to be a mind-reader? But you can't read his mind though. Would a "good thang" displace her emotions and blame her husband? Would a godly wife set different standards for her husband than she maintains for herself?
Are you to getting any of this?

The "good thang" has a certain character. Not only is she capable of maintaining a home and several businesses, but she has a certain personality as well. She is kind and considerate of her husband and everyone else. Now this is not to say that she is a pushover. Cause Lord knows, I am NOT! She is not that by any means. She picks her fights, so to speak. She doesn't have to go ghetto to get her point across. She is eloquent of speech, though able to break it down when she needs to.

She is dependable, accountable, reliable. She is interesting and engaging. She is encouraging and builds up rather than pulls down. She is wise. She is confident in the Lord first and then in herself. She is stable and steady. She has excellent communication skills and uses them proficiently. She isn't quick to judge. You are the good thang, that means you're not prone to flying off the handle. She doesn't make assumptions. It never ceases to amaze me how many women make assumptions about everything.

If they don't have an answer, they make one up to suit what they already believe. They believe a lie that they made up in their own head. And why is that always something negative? I know this may be a little hard to hear but if you don't know, then ask. Don't assume. If they can't tell you, have enough patience to help them tell you. You already know that many men are not verbal in how they express themselves. They aren't used to talking, much less talking about their feelings. Be patient. Be loving. Be there for them without jumping to conclusions and forcing them to explain themselves. Respect their process. You went through your process, allow him to go through his. If you create a safe place for them to talk, they will. But if every time you say you want to talk, it means they're about to get a beat down, you're going to get a shut down. They may show up but it's going nowhere. They have completely tuned right out. Try your best to be a soft place to land. Not a land mine. If you don't know how to communicate well, google ways to communicate. Develop a desire and passion to learn how to effectively communicate.

In addition, a good thang is disciplined in living her life. I don't mean regimented. Being regimented is like being religious. You know those church services where everything must happen at a certain time in a certain way. There is no leeway for a move of the Holy Ghost. He can't have his way in that kind of atmosphere. In fact, he's probably nowhere near that church. Being disciplined means being purposeful, being focused, being intentional. Makes sense right? A good thang is intentional and purposeful in her life. She's not a victim of circumstance and life isn't something that just happens to her.

The good thang is accountable for her behavior and choices. She says what she means and doesn't talk just to be talking. She is consistent in who she is. Not one way with one group and another way with someone else. People who know her trust her and know that her intention is never self-serving but she always means the best for everyone, even the ones that have done her wrong. She is transparent in her purpose and never has ulterior or hidden motives. I'm still talking about the good thang here.

The good thang is settled. She can be still and be at peace. She's grounded and a pleasure to be around. Her presence brings peace and life to the atmosphere. She is not attention-seeking, though ironically attracts attention with her very essence. Her joy and centeredness are like a magnet, she has an amazing power within. She draws positive results to her because she always thinks positively. She is not the kind of person that people walk on eggshells around, never knowing what response or reaction they'll get, always watchful of what mood she may be in.

There is absolutely nothing desperate about you Ms. GOOD THANG.

SINGLES let me say this to you, my queens.

Remember you reap what you sow. If you are sowing "I'm desperate for a man" seeds, you'll reap a harvest of men who will take advantage of that desperation. No no no, That's wifey energy. That's energy that just screams, "Use me, please!" and you are better and deserve better than that! You are not that girl anymore. Nope!

A good thang is secure. She has high self-esteem and values herself. She has confidence in GOD and in herself. She understands her self-awareness. Like I said, when we started, you have to know who you are. A good thang knows she's not perfect and neither is her husband. But she knows what her issues are and has handled them. They don't have to be completely gone either. We are all a work in progress. But God is enough to make up for any shortcomings we have when we surrender them to Him. When we know what areas we still struggle with, we also know when and how they pop up. If you need help working through your stuff, then talk to your pastor or seek out a Christian counselor. There is help out there, but you have to take the first step. Again… you must want it. The question is "Do you want it and how bad?"

A good thang is a good friend. She has healthy friendships that uplift and encourage her, and she them. She keeps appropriate confidences. She doesn't gossip and talk about people. She has healthy boundaries. She has goals even in her friendships. She has friends that support her and honor the relationship with her husband. She sees the best in them and they in her. They trust each other implicitly and completely.

A good thang can balance work and home. She places a priority on her time so that it is well spent. When she's working, she's working and when she's home, she's home. She is the authority on her family. She manages the home. She is attentive to the needs of each member and relates accordingly. If you are a mother, you know that each of your children is different and has different needs. One may be artistic, sensitive and contemplative while another may be precise, mathematical and decisive. Each requires a different language and way of parenting. They have different ways of hearing and relating to the world. A good thang is aware of and celebrates this uniqueness.

I'm telling you a good thang is mature, emotionally and spiritually. The Word says, "To whom much is given, much is required" (Luke 12:48). As a good thang, there may be things that she has to overlook for the sake of peace. There may be things that she has to choose to respond to rather than react to. According to the Word of God, she returns no one evil for evil (Romans 12:17). She's not vindictive. She is forgiving. She lives life from a space of centeredness, not being triggered up all the time. When you're triggered up, you are looking for a fight all the time. You're expecting it. And like a self-fulfilling prophecy, that is what happens. A good thang knows, by discernment, that when someone is angry, it may not be what it appears to be. They may be speaking from their own pain and disappointment. When someone lashes out at her, she may not be the real problem at all and is smart and grounded enough to know that. And to go a step further, she can help the other person see the truth about their anger. How awesome is that?! I think it's incredible! It is truly a gift to be a good thang.

This is part of the wisdom that a godly wife or good thang walks in. A definition of wisdom is having experience, knowledge and sound judgement. God's Word says for whoever lacks wisdom, to ask, and He will pour it out liberally (James 1:5). A good thang seeks the Lord's wisdom in her decisions, her relationships, her attitudes and her opinions. Her desire is to be a sound representation of Christ in her life, and that means that she thinks through the mind of Christ. She is not driven by her emotions. She chooses what she spends her time thinking about and casts down imaginations and everything that raises itself up as a standard against the knowledge of God. This means that she controls and guides her thoughts and emotions. She chooses joy. She doesn't just think up stupid stuff and act on it. She's not reactionary. She knows that just because she thought it does not make it true. That's part of knowing herself and where she still has challenges and weaknesses.

A good thang is kind. She is forgiving. She is thoughtful and considerate. A good thang knows God. She knows the sound of His voice and the move of His spirit. She is sensitive to the presence of God. She spends alone time with Him every day in her prayer closet and nurtures the relationship she has with Him. She regards Him in all that she does and holds her husband, family, business, church, decisions, and plans up before Him. She values His opinion and seeks His pleasure. She lives to hear Him say, "Well done, my Good and faithful servant. Enter into the joy of the Lord" (Matthew 25:21).

Seeing this description of a good thang may have just caused you to want to give up trying. You may be so overwhelmed by all of that that you want to just stop before you've even started! After all, who could possibly be all of that?! And if someone could, how long will it take to get there? I'll be honest, it feels impossible, however the remarkable part of all of this is that God is able to create all of this in you. I am a living witness. With all that I've been through, being this kind of woman certainly did not come naturally for me. I had to go through LIFE baby. God had to process me, crush me… just to produce oil. As I continued to walk with God and to surrender all of my hurt and pain to Him and to hold up this image of me before Him, over time, He re-created me to be more and more of this kind of woman. It was not something that I could have done on my own. It never even occurred to me that this was available. But what I know of the God I serve is that because this is His desire for me, it became the desire of my heart and He gave me the desire of my heart. I realize I didn't go through all this for nothing.

Remember I said that Shaun and I really had a hard time when we got together. Neither one of us was who we are today. We had a lot to let go of and a lot of healing to do. And we did it together. How?

Through learning to accept the imperfections in each other. We stopped making each other pay for what others did to us. Shaun and I learned to be very honest and not lie to spare feelings but really deal with the hard truths too. It's just how we say it. You know how the saying goes. "It's not what you say but how you say it." That is so true.

Being a godly wife doesn't mean DON'T SPEAK UP. It means to live the way GOD wants you to live.

What you also need to know is that when you desire to be a good thang, the man you desire changes too. If you really want to be this good thang we've been talking about, then certainly God will bless it and present you with a man of God. Remember, God created marriage and it is good in His sight. It's not about your master plan. It's about the plan of GOD concerning your life. Hey you GOOD THANG! I am proud of you. I believe that your heart and mind has already shifted. Let's go deeper.

11 BLENDED DRAMA

Oh SNAP!!! So here it is... The blended drama! You are happier than you've ever been. See... here it is, you met the man of your dreams, you get to know all the things about him, now love's in sight and you even accepted the fact that he has a child or children, because that's not a deal breaker for you anymore. I want to acknowledge here... not everybody will have children from a prior relationship, but there is a percentage of you that probably will be in this situation. This chapter is for you! Keep reading my dears.

Ok, you and he are excited about life and you know that he is the one! I mean you are ready to go to the next level with him and live happily ever after. Oh, but what about the child(ren) and most of all what about their mother? The child(ren) have taken a strong liking to you and you have a deep regard as well. Where do you go from here? Are you prepared for what this is? What does this really mean? Are you ready to be an instant mom to kids you didn't have? Now I will say this, not all blended families are suffering. Some are beautiful, we see some great blended families and they're doing very well. Not all blended families have issues but there are a lot of families that do and I'm going to share a few stories of what I believe is this blended drama. I had a conversation with my husband before he and I were married and my stepdaughter (My bonus baby) was one and a half at the time. She is a beautiful chocolate baby and I knew that Shaun, who was my boyfriend then, and I were going to be in a committed relationship and that meant if I was in a committed relationship with him that I would have to be in a committed relationship with her too! His daughter was just as important to me as he was.

Unfortunately, her mother who didn't know a thing about me didn't have a strong regard for me at all, honey. Ok… so she hated me. His child's mother and I did not get along at all. We were not friends, we weren't trying to be friends either. This woman hated the fact that their pattern of "I can have you back at will" was broken and this was before I came into his life as his lady. I didn't break up a happy home, as a matter of fact she and Shaun had broken before I came into the picture. Now I can hear some of you right now saying "but Markita you broke up their happy home!" No way did I do that. They were not in a committed relationship and when Shaun began to have feelings for me they were not involved sexually either. Again, the woman didn't even know me not to like me. Lord when I tell you some of the things that you are about to read will have you flipping through these pages! I promise you this is not to shame anyone because I did not always respond or do things right to her either. I think looking back maybe I could've handled things a little better but hey this is the REAL RAW UNKUT truth here.

You know I was raised to walk away and turn the other cheek when people offend you, hurt you, talk about you etc., but some of the things this woman did to me was going to put me in jail! Yes, the woman of GOD was going to catch a charge!

Picture it, imagine someone calling your phone over 100 times not in a day but within two hours! Imagine someone calling your job and lying on you for no reason! Imagine someone that you don't even know trying to sabotage your social media influence, before social media got real big, I'm talking about in the "Myspace" days. You guys... it was awful, but I endured it because I loved her child and my boyfriend. I could've walked away and not dealt with him or baby girl anymore, but that's not what God showed me, and we just had to endure. Now listen... don't get me wrong... of course there were times when I blamed Shaun for this awful behavior and I wanted him to get her together but how could I expect him to get her together? If she didn't respect him she wasn't going to do anything that he said and certainly not give a crap about me as far she can see me.

The chaos and interruptions were constant, and we almost gave up on each other many times because of the damage she tried to cause in our relationship... all because she was angry. (Let me drop this BONUS in this, to all of you wives or girlfriends that want to be with a man that has children, you must understand that he had a past with this person. In the past, it wasn't always bad times.

Look here... there had to be some good times, or the child wouldn't be here. Even if it was just sex and the child(ren) were brought into the world, you must understand you are dealing with a spirit of rejection and anger.)

So as time went on a whole lot of other things have transpired and our daughter was getting older and by this time I'm pregnant with our son... meanwhile Shaun and I were still battling through this drama... this whole BLENDED DRAMA! I wanted to be a good stepmother to my daughter and I know that she loved me but there were times where she would even say "I don't have to listen to you because my mommy said..." and it would break my heart. I taught her how to tie her shoes... I potty trained her and when she would have bad dreams and she stayed with her father, I was there with her. I never loved her less than my own new baby boy and it was a struggle because this little girl looks just like her mother. I witnessed the scrutiny and the frustration of seeing my husband suffer wanting to be with his child and that was taken from him because the mother is angry. I mean could you imagine the arguing and just plain disrespect. Let me tell you... it's hell... there's nothing fun about it but God will give you the peace in knowing that it's going to work out! It's going to work out for your good and ultimately your family.

You don't let anyone tear up your new family. You don't let outside people become inside people and, even yourself, sabotage what you believe GOD has purposed for you. To all the ladies that choose to be in a relationship with men who have children, it is not their fault that they are here, and you chose to be with their father. Now you must love them unconditionally no matter what and be a great mother figure still.

No, not all the baby mothers are always bad guys either. For those of you that never got the respect you deserve, I would like to apologize on behalf of all the wives and new girlfriends that have made it hard for you to have peace with your baby father. To all of you wives that get a kick out of a man not spending time or supporting his children that are not with you, shame on you! Be a woman of integrity that brings it to his attention so that no matter what he is supposed to care and support his children, no matter what. It's a fact that you're not going to always get along. You're not going to always see eye to eye, and guess what, you don't have to be her friend, but you must love those children.

Thus, the reason why your husband is with you is because God had him find you! He is not with her for a reason and it's not that she was so terrible... consider this... maybe he was terrible, and things changed. This is going to be hard for some of you to read but I have to say it. Think about if the shoe was on the other foot. What if you were the one that was with him and had his children, helped him when he was down, loved him even when you didn't love yourself, but you did your best to only see him mature or maybe not mature, he decided to move on and no longer deal with you and then he gives another woman what you waited for.

How would it make you feel? It should make you feel some compassion. I know for me that's exactly what happened. To see how GOD totally turned my husband around was amazing. It was

work and a process that I went through with him.
Ultimately the best thing I did was to allow Jesus to
show him Christ. I had to speak life into a man that
felt like the bottom of his shoes. He was so
wounded. Not just by her, but other women, and
this was the last for him. I told him He was violated
by her words, why? She was hurting too. Now, I am
not justifying the mess that happened, but I
understood this is all warfare! Warfare I didn't like at
all. I had to put myself on the outside and look in.
You must do that too. I promise you it will help a
great deal.

Baby mother, I must encourage you. Life
happens, but if you are a bitter woman and you have
not forgiven your boyfriend or ex-husband, it's hard
for you to see him happy. That's not a "him" thing,
my dear… that's something that's going on inside of
you that only God can heal, and I don't care if you
get married and have other babies, have a career,
move out of state or whatever. Until you can forgive
him, he's always going to be inside of you. Your

children are always going to be a reminder of him. Baby Mother, you must rise above that and move on with your life and let him be a father if he wants to be.

If he doesn't want to be a father, don't make him. Notice I said father, not your best pal or lover. God Will take care of you and I've witnessed this firsthand with aunts, cousins and God sisters who deal with blended drama and baby daddy issues too and I've seen them raise their children and not miss a beat, they lack for nothing. I've seen women forgive these men and not hold them responsible any longer for their own happiness.

I'm not telling you this because I'm a wife... I'm telling you this because I'm a woman and I believe in you and I believe in your potential. Baby mother, I believe that God does not want you to be full of rage and bitterness. I believe that if you release the man from your heart and not hate him anymore, not to want to see him suffer the more because you two are not together... that God will bless you. God will give you the desires of your heart.

It wasn't until my ex-husband had a child while we were just freshly divorced, that I was angry at a woman that I didn't even know. I was bitter at a woman that had nothing to do with the choices he made. You see, I thought my problem was with him when I realized the problem would never go anywhere until I released him and that's exactly what I did. I released him out of my heart I moved on with my life. That may be hard for you to do but I'm telling you now you can do it.

Blended drama can be very dangerous. I've seen people get hurt physically, emotionally, and financially too. I've seen court cases dragged out and I've seen the court systems not go in the man's favor when he did do right, and the Baby mother was DEAD wrong. I've witnessed men cry and breakdown because they really want to be in their child's life and just want peace in the home. They just want to love their kids.

So, ladies that are with men with children that are not "yours" remember what your assignment is. You're the help meet. Help him be strong. Help him not to give up on seeing his kids. Help him to be the best father he can be. Remind him that the battle isn't his, it is the Lord's! You can do it! I had to, many other women had to as well.

One day when I saw my husband cry over his daughter, I told him "honey, she won't be little forever… she's going to grow up. She is going to remember how you treated her and how I treated her. She's going to remember the love that she got from my side of the family and your side of the family and no matter what her mother does, it will still never outweigh the truth."

I want to encourage all women who may be dealing with the bad side of the blended drama hold on. The truth is going to come out and the child will remember. That's why you must be a woman of peace no matter what. Yes, you want to retaliate… yes, you want to fight… yes, you want to expose them… yes, you want to ignore the child and no, you don't want to pay extra after paying child support.

You do it because God is keeping good records, you do it because God wants you to be a woman of wisdom, he wants you to be integral… he wants you to be an example of what a favored woman you are and that he found you to be the good thing. So, your husband or your fiancé needs you to be his peace… in the situation… not a headache… not a nagger. He needs you to help him strategize… he need you to pray for him and pray for the baby mother too! That's right and do not pray for her demise, pray that GOD gives her peace. You would want somebody to pray for you right?

I asked GOD to give me a revelation about our situation, and about her, in particular. Guess what He showed me? Shaun never apologized for his part. I was blown away, I thought to myself, that was years ago, but GOD showed me how that offense was so deep because He not only moved on, but in her mind, he was moving on and leaving his daughter behind and she wouldn't have the life that I have with him and the children we have together. She really felt that she was dismissed. I had to tell my husband that. I promise you I didn't want to tell him that, but I had too. He received it and apologized to her. That was the right thing to do. Now, in no way am I suggesting that you're to bow down and overly extend yourself while constantly being disrespected. Baby father, you can't be the answer and the problem. You must draw limitations and boundaries. Ask God for wisdom with that. Include your wife/fiancé… that woman you chose to build the rest of your life with. Don't let her feel like an outcast. You are a team, and the baby mother doesn't have a choice with that. This must be taught, and consistency is key. Communication is necessary. Prayer and coming into agreement is not an option. That's the only way this works.

Now this isn't everyone's life. I've also seen where it did work… holidays spent with each other, birthday parties coming together and there's no animosity. The families have put a system together that works and they celebrating as one, so don't think that it's not possible. All things are possible through Christ!

My truth is though, there were times with my GOD - fearing, anointed self, when I wanted to put his child's mother through a wall (and almost did but don't tell nobody!). All for the things she did, not only to my husband, but to me. I had to remember "Baby girl is not going to be 2, 4, 6, 8, 10 forever… You keep loving the gift GOD gave you and remember Markita, this is not just about you." It's about how the kids are affected too. If GOD didn't think you could handle it, you wouldn't be where you are now.

You may not ever have this "Kum ba ya" moment, everybody gets along and are besties. And that is ok. One thing I know for sure is it's an honor to be a mother, even to a child I didn't birth, and there is NO DRAMA that can come between the bond that me, my husband, and all our children have. We are a family that is blended, yes, but we are family no doubt!

12 REAL Q & A

"I am called to ministry and my husband isn't.
What should I do?"
Well... He is called to ministry. He is called to cover
you. We, as wives, need to understand that is the
first ministry in family. Our husbands are the
authority of the home and family. So, you see, he
may not be a preacher or prophet to the world but
he should be all those things to you. What you
should do is always respect and honor him. Pray...
and I mean pray... for your husband. Treat him the
way God teaches us how to. Remember, he is
sanctified by you, his wife. Keep speaking life to him

and never put another man above your husband, no matter his level of depth in God.

"Can I propose to my boyfriend?"

GIRL! Where are you right now so I can shake you?! He who finds a wife! Not she who finds a husband. At the end of the day, you want God's ways and his methods. You are not the spiritual authority. Asking for a hand in marriage is about leading. What you want to lead him for, unless it's leading him to Jesus. So, I would not recommend you getting on your pretty knee to ask a man to marry you.

"Should I stay in a physically abusive marriage?" Absolutely NOT! Get out of there! If you are not getting help and he is not getting help or he is not changing, you need to leave that situation. Can God restore anything? Absolutely He can. Can God turn a man's heart from cheating? Absolutely. But it is not the will of God that you be verbally, physically, emotionally abused. God will take care of you. I know that. You need a plan and surround yourself with people that will support your decision to leave something that is toxic and dangerous.

"Should we pray for desired intimacy with our future husband?"

Marriage is a gift. God honors marriage between husband and wife; sex is the gift! You want to have a great time with your spouse. The marriage bed is undefiled. People in the world have more sex than married couples and they feel free! We that are under "holy" matrimony should express pure passion and intimacy with our spouses. You should be excited about having a relationship with your husband. God created sex for marriage. He knows

."I am single and abstaining from sex. Should I just masturbate?"

Ok, masturbation is self-gratification, lustful, and perverted. You shouldn't do that because it opens a gateway or a door to other things that are demonic. Such as pornography, slipping back into fornication. What you can do is get an accountability partner, someone you trust and who will pray with you and also listen when you need support. Read your bible, and always embrace the fruits of the spirit. (Galatians 5:22-23)

But the fruit of the Spirit is love, joy, peace, longsuffering, gentleness, goodness, faith, Meekness, temperance (self-control): against such there is no law. You will not bow down to this fleshly desire and sinful nature. It will not control you.

"I still love my ex-husband. Should I tell him or just wait on the Lord to change his heart?"

Ok that is a great question. You can be honest with him and let him know how you feel. That's what adults do. Now if he is no longer interested or wanting to reconcile, you have to move on. That is his choice. I have seen people go through divorce and later they did get back together, and all is well. So, if it is meant to be, it will be. In the meantime, move forward and don't waste time wanting somebody if they don't want you.

"Do we need to denounce rape and molestation?"

Yes. Because when you have been violated and forced to do things against your will, there is a spirit of rejection and shame that will try to humiliate you and make you feel like it was your fault. It wasn't your fault. So that is another trap of the enemy. It's deception and so you denounce that and come against it. How do I know? Because I was raped and molested. And I had to get that image out of my spirit. So, I can talk about it freely because I am free. I'm able to identify with women who have gone through that because I've overcome it. I don't let that become a place of shame. I've overcome it and I'm victorious. Denounce that spirit. Don't feel dirty anymore. You're not dirty. That was not God's will. God didn't want that to happen to you. That was a sick person that was full of demons that did that to you and it was not your fault! Say that out loud: "It was not my fault!" Say it again... now say it again: "It was not my fault!" God was not in that. But He promised us that whatever the enemy meant for our bad He would turn it around for our good. So absolutely denounce rape and molestation. And I decree and declare: Father, we thank you for freeing us from the shame of rape and the shame of molestation, being forced to do things at a young age or at any age. And we never told anybody, or we told people and they didn't believe us, or they believed us but there were no consequences. God, I thank you right now for the freedom to move on from that and for the freedom to be healed as a testimony to be a blessing for someone else at the appointed time. In Jesus' name, amen. Be free from that. Don't let that cripple you another day. You will function. You will trust men, you will not think of that person on top of you again. You will not think of that person who rubbed your breast and made you do things you should not have been doing. You will not be crippled by that. Not another day.

"I have children with the person that I still struggle to not reminisce about every now and then. I know we weren't on the same page but sometimes

I think back. I have to see him because of the children. How do I get past it?"

You still have an attachment with this person. When you have kids with someone you get connected with them. It does not mean that it has to be a spiritual attachment. It does not have to be a spiritual connection. So, you have to go through the steps I outlined earlier. Worship. Repent. Denounce that person: "God I respect this person. He is the father of my children. I care about this individual. But I don't want to be stuck in yesteryear with this person." And please, whatever you do, don't fall and sleep with him because he's your children's father. Remain pure before the Lord and He will bring you a husband that will love you and your kids. Don't fall for that kind of trap. "Teach me Lord, how to co-parent with him without lusting for him." Worship, repent, denounce. Say his name out loud. "Father, I thank you for taking the spirit of so-and-so out of my heart. I don't want every time he comes over for something to leap in me. Every time I see him something jumps in me." That's not God. That's your flesh. So don't get caught up and don't go the other way either. Don't hate him. You chose him.

"If only I would have waited. I got married and could have been married to the man that God had for me. I listened to others when I got pregnant." What you have to do is forgive yourself. And forgive the people that you are resenting right now. You have to forgive them because they thought they were doing what was best for you. But the Word says that what the enemy meant for our harm, God can turn around for our good. So, I want you to think about all the great times you've had with these children and grandchildren. Ask God to help you recover and heal in those places that you still hurt. What I know about God is that He already knows how we feel, so we can't be afraid to tell him how we feel. We have to not be afraid to tell him how we feel. To share this hurt with Him. I don't understand this. I don't like this. He said be angry and sin not. His ways are above our ways. He has ways that we don't know about… we have to walk this thing out. Maybe life went this way to prevent you from going through something else. Just maybe. Embrace the journey that you went on. I want you to feel good about how you mothered these children and how you're an amazing grandmother. Do not allow the enemy to trick you into thinking you wasted time. Don't ever allow the enemy to make you think you have wasted time. Because God is a redeemer of time. The redeemer of time, He said we can recover. He'll replenish. He'll restore. Begin to think about those years and what you've endured and thank God that you were their mother. Thank Him that what you went through didn't kill you. I pray God will heal you in those places you hide so very well.

"I have insecurities because I am divorced and have six children. It holds me back. Even though I have a lot to bring to the table, it holds me back."

God gave you those children because he trusted you. You didn't ask to go through a divorce. You didn't ask to be dropped and rejected. You didn't ask to have these children by yourself. It's not fair that you have six children now and you have to raise them. God never wanted that for you. But He does trust you to raise them. He is so awesome that He will still send you a man who can't have children. You need to hear me in the Holy Ghost. He can send you a man that wants children and who can't have them. What you have to do is start bringing him forward: "God I thank you for the husband that you have sent me. I thank you that he's gonna love me and adore me and accept these as his children. God I thank you for preparing me and teaching me how to live with a man that didn't have children. Or who may have children and we are going to live harmoniously. We are going to break the stigma and blended families can get along. Thank you that my sons and daughters don't give me a hard time because mama has moved on. That they will have another father figure in their life." There are people out there who have a whole lot of kids and they still get remarried, and they embrace all the children as their own. We declare now that they will be your portion. God will send you a husband to care for you and for your children. And that they will receive him as a father and that it won't be hard. Bring no random men around your children until you know he's the one. Keep random men away from your babies. You will know he is the one. They should not see mama with random men. Don't limit God. He is able to send someone to you that will love you and your children. Unconditionally. I have an oldest daughter. I didn't give birth to her but she's mine, everywhere we go people say, "Your daughter looks just like you." I love this little girl so much that she has taken on aspects of me. I've known her since she was one year old. And I've cared for her as my first child. So, I love her as if I had her out of my own belly. So, there are men out there that will love you and your children. But you have got to love him and his children if he has children.

How do I help my Christian friends and family that are living in the wifey situation without coming across as judgmental?

Tell them this: "God never wanted that for you. He never wanted you to be somebody's wifey, "Booh" or "Bae." And you got to be able to tell them that you love them. At the end of the day, people are going to do what they want to. You can't force them. But you have a duty and obligation to tell them when they are in error. "I love you. You deserve better. It's not that he's a bad guy. You just keep thinking that one day he's gonna wake up and carry you away and he's not. You're not doing it God's way. You're doing it your way and you're praying that God will bless it. Okay, so I go into a store and I shoplift. And I take some clothes and stuff them in a bag and pray that nobody catches me. Please God don't let anybody see me. Please don't let anybody catch me. Please God bless me with these clothes. It's illegal and you're going to jail!" And you want God to bless it. Please God bless this relationship. No, He's not. And if He does you are headed for rocky times, for sure. And marriage is already hard. It's already work and war in marriage. It comes with the package. So when you are disobedient, and out of order and out of God's way and his timing and all of that would add more trouble to it. So, if you see a freight train headed at these people and you tell them to get off the tracks and they don't, then you have done your job. You have done what you were supposed to do and you keep it moving. You can't make people change their minds. You just present them with the truth. And that's not being judgmental. Being judgmental is this: "You going to hell if you don't stop. God ain't in that and you going to hell." There is a way to say it: "I'm really concerned. I'm really worried about you. I'm concerned. I don't think this is cool and I don't think this is right. I'm really going to be praying for you. This is not God's will. I love you." Always come back with compassion. "I love you. I'm just concerned." They will either receive you or not. Just love them.

"I've always been told I'm ugly. It keeps me from being everywhere and with everyone. But no one knows. I thought I was in love."
Right now, let me cancel out the lie... you are beautiful. I was told as a kid "you're ugly, you're fat, you're this, you're that. You're not light enough; your hair is not long enough; your teeth have gaps; you have a big butt," whatever. We have to cancel out the lies; the Bible says that we are fearfully and wonderfully made. I wish somebody would look me in my face and tell me I'm ugly. You must be smoking a new brand of crack. Look at yourself in the mirror and tell yourself, "I'm beautiful. There is something about every woman that is beautiful. It may be your eyes, cheekbones, bone structure, hips, breasts, legs, feet, hands, whatever, there is something beautiful about every last one of us. And you have to tap in to that place that no matter what anyone tells you, you know you are gorgeous. And

another thing is that a little gloss never hurt anybody. A little bronzer on the cheek. A little mascara. I've seen some less attractive women have makeovers and there is something about a pallet and a brush. Maybe you need to budget yourself and go to the department store makeup counter and have a makeover. I challenge some of you to do that. Go learn how to apply it to enhance your features. Take yourself to a Lancôme or a Mac counter and get some help. Stop watching YouTube if you don't know what you're doing. If they offer you samples, accept them. Don't buy anything if you can't afford it. Get your face done, take some pictures. Keep it in your phone, put it on social media, and say I just had a makeover. Put it up and look at it. See how beautiful you are. I don't want you thinking all the stars on TV are natural... now keep in mind... I like to enhance my beauty, but I am not trying so hard that without those things I can't be recognized and scare y'all! but that is weave; that is lashes; that is airbrush; that is Botox; that is contouring; that is tattooed eyebrows; that is snatched noses; that is all fake or enhanced (Whatever makes you feel better). We're talking about butt pads, colored contacts, butt lifts, liposuction, implants, stage makeup, pounds of makeup. Bleaching skin. This is professional makeup applied professionally. What are you comparing yourself to? Who told you that you were ugly? Compared to who? I know girls that had to have their legs amputated trying to get butt implants. They allowed the media to tell them that the new body is a snatched waist and a round behind. If you weren't born with it, embrace what it is. Do some squats or not. And yes, the celebrities do have low self-esteem. I watched a video on people who are celebrities that have so much money they could wipe their behinds with it; they have so much and yet they are depressed and suicidal. They can buy anything, any house, any car, even friends and they're depressed. I believe they are depressed even from childhood. I still remember the things that people from my childhood said about me. Watch this.

Those are the same people that need my help today, I say that not being boastful or arrogant. I had to heal in order to help some of them for real. Those are the same people who look twice their age and I don't. They come to me so I can mother them. They come to me for prayer now. They come to me for the sister love that moves them back to where they need to be. I was never the pretty girl in the 6th, 7th, or 8th grade. And now, when I see the girls that were the pretty girls, I wonder what happened? The same people who do you wrong are the same people that will need you.

"How do I let go of the feelings of loving a married man after I've said no and let go?" First thing, repent and forgive yourself for loving someone who did not belong to you. It was very brave of you to ask this question. Thank you for your trust. You know I will not judge you or give you false information. Let me say this: you are human. You have emotions and you have feelings. It was not right. It was absolutely positively wrong.

However, you are human and we are bound to make mistakes. You also need to be transformed by the renewing of your mind. According to Romans 12:2 "And be not conformed to the world: but be ye transformed by the renewing of your mind, that ye may prove what is that good and acceptable and perfect will of God."

We break from those things through the blood of Jesus. You cared for that person and you lay down with him and had sex with him and an exchange of souls took place. And even though now you say you are done with him, you have to ask God to release you from any ungodly ties to him. And this is for anyone. Say out loud, "I denounce the spirit of so-and-so and I release them in Jesus' name." And you gotta do that every day until the very thought of that person does not cause your womb to leap; it doesn't cause you to have a reaction to them. I've been there so I'm not judging you. I was involved with a married man and I loved him. This is for anyone that you are involved with that does not belong to you; you have to let them go from your mind and spirit. You get rid of stuff. Clothing, shoes, jewelry, pictures and emails and all of that. Don't pay him back by talking to his wife. Don't expose anybody. Just ask God to take this from me, get him out of me. And do it as often as you think of him and as long as you have a reaction to the thought of him. "God get him out of me. Get him out."

Now, the following is a list of questions for you to ask yourself while you wait for your spouse. You have to be honest. Nobody is looking at you while you answer these questions. They can help you prepare for what's next. If you are already married, take some time with your spouse to answer these questions as honestly as you can. There is no wrong answer. Truthful answers can improve and strengthen your relationship. They are not designed to be answered easily or quickly. They should stir up thoughts about areas where you may still be holding on to the past. If you are answering them with your husband, as you go through the questions, be sensitive that some things you may need to share here could be hurtful in the hearing of them. Take your time and get through this part one question at a time. Ready?

1. Can I identify when I was happiest in my life? What was happening then that made me feel such happiness? Is any of that still happening for me now?

2. Do I have issues with my parents that I have not healed from?

3. Do I know what I need from a man? Or do I expect him to know?

4. Are there areas of my life that I intentionally withhold from my boyfriend/partner/husband? What are they and what makes me intentionally keep them from him?

5. What about intimacy scares me?

6. Can I love unconditionally? Can I love me just the way I am? Can I love someone else just the way they are?

7.   Are there unspoken deal-breakers for me in relationships? If so, what are they?

8.   Are there things that I will not compromise on?

9.   What does "love" mean to me? What does being "in love" mean?

10.   Have I considered his process too?

11.   Do I feel connected to my partner? Is there anything that would make me feel more connected?

12.   What concerns me most about life? What am I most afraid of?

13.   What do I want my life to look like? Do I feel that I am moving in that direction? If not, what needs to be different?

14.   When I think about marriage, what do I expect it to be like? Is that what's happening in my marriage now?

15.   Is there anything that I feel unfulfilled about in my life? Is there a way to feel more fulfilled?

16.   Is my relationship satisfying to me? What would I like to be better? What would I just like to be different?

17.   Are there times when I don't feel respected in my relationship? If so, when is that?

18.   What makes me angry?

19.   Can I love a man that has children?

20.   How do I handle my anger?

21.   Am I honest about how I really feel about myself?

22.   Do I have what it takes to be an "Instant mom"?

23.   Am I living where I want to live? Am I living the way I want to live?

24.   What brings me joy?

25.   What are my challenges to intimacy? How to do I deal with them?

26.   What do I think are the husband's responsibilities?

27.   What do I think are the wife's responsibilities?

28. How would I want to address chores and daily living needs like dinner preparation and cooking, grocery shopping, oil changes for the car or cars, etc.?

29. How do I think money should be handled in the family? By whom and how?

30. What does submission really mean to me?

31. Is there a "Breadwinner?" If so, who is it?

32. How do I need to be shown love? "I feel loved when _____."

33. Do I want to reconcile with my ex? Can I move pass the past?

34. How do I want to include friends in my relationship? How do they fit?

35. What do I want to have in common with my husband?

36. In my relationships, do I usually give more than I receive? Is that okay? What do I need to do to change that? Are my relationships one-sided with me giving more than I receive?

37. Are my needs being met in my relationship? If not, which are not? Can they be? How?

38. Have I sought God about my relationship or have I been doing what I want to do?

39. Have I prayed for my husband? (even if he hasn't come yet).

40. Do I feel closer to God because of this relationship? Does it make me want to be closer to God?

41. Does this relationship encourage my growth in Christ?

42. Are there issues in my relationship that need to be addressed before I feel comfortable moving forward?

43. Do I have unfinished business from my past that has to be addressed before I feel I can move forward?

44. Am I staying in this relationship to rescue my friend? Am I playing caretaker?

45. Am I afraid of who I see in the mirror? What is staring back at me?

46. Am I staying in this relationship because I don't want to hurt my friend's feelings?

47. Why do I want to get married?

48. Could I be just as happy if I stayed single?

49. Have I ever been abused? Physically, sexually, emotionally, or verbally? Who did I share it with? What was their response? What do I need now?

50. How do I make decisions?

51. What would I be willing to give up to have a successful, happy marriage?

52. What makes me feel safe?

53. Who makes me feel safe?

54. Who is responsible for my failed relationships? Me? Or them? Or both of us?

55. Do I feel like I have to change for this relationship to work?

56. Do I wear rejection like a badge of honor?

57. Do I have to win arguments? What happens if I lose?

58.   Are there red flags that I'm ignoring? Am I willing to hear from wise counsel about any red flags? (Addictions, unfaithfulness, history of being an abuser or of being abused, different spiritual beliefs, conflict and aggression, poor communication, etc.)

59.   Do I have secrets?

60.   Are we friends first, then spouses? If not, how can we build a stronger friendship?

61.   How much do I trust my husband? How can we build more trust, stronger trust?

62.   Can I trust myself to be honest with myself?

63.   What am I watching and listening to? Is it helping me to grow or not?

64.   Who can tell me "No"? When I need to be corrected who's no do I trust?

65.   Do I believe in love at first sight? Why or why not.

66.   Can I go from courting to marriage?

13 *THE ELEPHANT*

So, let's talk about this divorce thing. I know a lot of people who are considering, going through or are now divorced. I want to pray with you and I want to encourage you along the way concerning divorce.

Divorce is not easy, and it is not something that we as Christians should enjoy, we should not celebrate it at all. This is very hard because you do feel the grief from literally severing a connection, breaking a connection, a covenant, unknitting a bond, and ripping a contract up with someone that you vowed to be with for the rest of your life and so I don't take this lightly at all.

Being a divorced woman myself, I know firsthand the grief and pain that is literally indescribable. I know that it wasn't God's will, no... let me rephrase that, it wasn't God's perfect will for me although he allowed it to be so. I made it! I overcame! I am more than what the enemy said I would be; broken, unloved, tampered with, rejected, not worthy to be a wife. All LIES!

Truth is that sometimes we marry the "wedding ceremony" and get to know the person later. We get so excited about the dress and tux that we forget we have to live together after we say "I do". For some the 2nd, 3rd and even 4th time. I tell people that if you just want a ring and a dress, go to the bridal store put your favorite dream dress on. Put on a tiara, take a few pictures and then take the dress off and go home. It sounds funny, but I am serious. Don't be so focused on the wedding that you marry a stranger. You married a fairytale and never asked God first. You asked God after you made up your mind to do what you wanted, as most of us do, and then the reality sets in that you don't know what you've gotten yourself into. After the honeymoon and the sex is over, are you really ready to spend the rest of your life with your spouse? If you were cheating before and didn't stop, marriage isn't going to fix it. If you had a spending problem before and didn't get help, marriage isn't going to stop it. If you had problems with communicating and working out problems before and didn't resolve it, marriage isn't going to fix that. Marriage amplified and magnified what you tried to hide. Does that make sense to you?

There's always that feeling, that sign and that's GOD warning and trying to show you to either wait or RUN! Ask yourself did you ignore the signs?

Let's be clear… women hurt, and men hurt too. We must be honest about the help we need with this topic that's not always addressed with clarity, and practicality. Some things you and I are not going to just shout and spin our way through. We need to talk it out. We need the truth. We need answers. We need wise counsel, not made up or false hope, during these times.

I want to answer a few questions that were sent to me. I want to share some truth moments and I also want to give you some nuggets and wisdom on what to do before during and after divorce! No, I am not a psychiatrist or therapist, but I am a woman that has experience and wisdom. It is my heart's desire to see you whole and no longer walking around pretending. As sure as I type this I am asking GOD to give me the words to say to you. Let's begin with a word of prayer.

"God in the name of Jesus, I just thank you right now for this moment in time a time of reflecting a time of facing our reality in our truth. Lord, you want us to be free and liberated from all shame, all humiliation, all fear, and abuse associated with divorce. Lord, we know that divorce is not something that you celebrate but we thank you for peace in knowing that all things are working together for our good and for us that are called according to your purpose. We thank you Lord that even in divorce there is love, there is life, and there is joy!

Father, I pray for everyone that is going through divorce or that is divorced and those that are in the middle of separation that you would give them peace, the peace of God that surpasses all their natural understanding. I intercede on their behalf right now and I thank you that you're going to turn their mourning into dancing. I thank you for giving them beauty from ashes. I believe that you're going to allow them to be put back together again. I pray for the families that are being affected by divorce and separation. I lift the children up to you. I pray for the hearts of the people that have been torn apart, God, that you would mend and heal. God, that you would begin to restore the joy back into their lives because the joy of the Lord is their strength. I dismantle every word curse and every cycle of patterns that will cause sabotage in your marriage. I come against Break ups and separation that are not in your plan for your sons and daughters. We know that divorce at times is necessary, however we don't wear divorce as a badge of honor, but we thank you that we are overcomers and we thank you that we are victorious, even in divorce. Father, I thank you that we will not be ashamed to say that we were once married and no longer married. I thank you for those people who are searching themselves and they are no longer lonely, and I thank you for sending resources and help and answers to them now. God, in the name of Jesus, I pray that you would cover and protect those who may be running for their very lives. Danger is following them, and divorce is their only way of escape. Give strategies now. Let them not look back but move and press forward. Lord, I thank you for turning every stony heart back into flesh. I pray God that you would begin to show them the light at the end of the tunnel I thank you that there is a silver lining in the cloud. I so want to thank you Lord that their frowns are being turned upside down. I thank you that families will come together and support them. I thank you for their prayer partners and accountability partners coming into their lives. Father I thank you that they will not be fearful to trust and love again. I decree and declare in the name of Jesus that your perfect will be made manifest regarding relationships and future marriage if that is your plan. We break ties and demonic attachments now! We bind up anger and rage and loose love and peace! God thank you that we will not be afraid to share our circumstances and our testimonies. God, I am so excited for I know you can be trusted! If it's your will for the people who have gone through divorce to be remarried to the person that they divorced, then God I pray for a clean slate that you would bring forth new eyes and a new heart and that forgiveness will take place and there will be no digging up from the past. I even bless you for a fresh anointing on all new marriages and I thank you for those people that are single that they fall in love with you all over again and that they are excited about growing and about loving themselves first! Lord we just praise you right now and we just thank you and we give you the honor! You're worthy of it and we love you and we trust you in Jesus name amen."

"Markita, I can't get over my ex-husband. What should I do?"

Well here is the thing. You loved and made a vow and commitment to someone that you are no longer with. Though you went through a natural divorce he is still inside of you. You must break every attachment from your heart, mind, and soul. You must be unknitted. Be honest and ask the Lord to search your heart. Take it one moment at a time. Start with daily confessions that you are free from him. That you are no longer bound to him. Please forgive him too. This is not strange, it's normal, but the more you move forward and not look back the better it gets. Praying. Fasting. All that helps too. Be consistent with this. Better days are ahead.

"Markita, should I remain close to my in-laws?" Now I am going to be super honest. It was a no for me. But every situation isn't the same. I would say boundaries are in order. You have to remember that's still his/her family first. Unless you have children together, I would use wisdom in conversation as to information being shared. My ex father-in-law and one sister in-law was awesome, but my ex mother-in-law and her crew were pure evil. I had to detach from them all, because that was his family. When we divorced there were no children and so I had no reason other than being familiar to want to stay connected to that family. I had to

choose my sanity over my love for a couple of them.
It wasn't worth it to me.

"Markita, this is my 3rd failed marriage and I want to hurry and date again. Is that wrong?"
Honey, slow down. Don't be like the woman at the well that met Jesus. In a hurry to get married when you really need healing and avoid running into relationships because you're afraid of being lonely. I know that people feel to get over one person is to hurry and be with the next, but why be unfair to yourself that way? You deserve time. Time to reflect, time to get to know you again, time to get the prior ones out of your heart. You shouldn't want any more cycles of failed marriage. Marriage is not the answer, God is. Make a vow to the Lord and let him process and deliver you. Want him more than you want marriage.

"Markita, my church leaders told me I was wrong for leaving my marriage. I shouldn't split

up my family. But I have been cheated on and he/she won't stop."

I would never tell you to go against your beliefs. I will say this, God hates divorce. However, biblically you have grounds for divorce when adultery is taking place. If he/she refused to stop you had a right to leave that toxic relationship. Prayer can do a lot of things but if the heart is not willing to change and there is no repenting, you have to do what you have to do... for the sake of your kids. They shouldn't see dysfunction right in their face. By your staying with someone who dishonors GOD and you, you're teaching your kids that this is ok and it's not. This is something you must free yourself from. What are you freeing yourself from? Explaining yourself to people about what's healthy and right for your family. You wouldn't think twice about protecting your kids from anybody else that would cause emotional damage. Why are you second guessing it now? I didn't say they should stop loving the other parent but being in the same house? Maybe no.

Markita, Can I still have sex with my ex? I know him, and I don't want to sleep around."

Umm. You can do whatever you want to do beloved. You will never get over him. And yes, it is wrong. You two are no longer married, so it's fornication!! Yes, you are taking 10 steps backwards sleeping with your ex. You're comfortable (too comfortable) and why would you want to open the door to that pain again? He doesn't belong to you and you don't belong to him. This is a dangerous game you are playing, and nobody wins. Ask God to keep your body. You are not a slave to sex!

"Markita, I am ready to love again after 5 years of being single. What should I do?"

You should know that you're ready to date again. Ask God to do a quick thing baby! Cause you're a "GOOD THANG" and it can go from courting to marriage! God is good like that. You don't have time to waste. Make sure you learned from your last marriage. Don't get in a hurry and you're not free. Now, only you know that truth. Be open to love and be open to trust. Don't make the past mistakes and remember you are asking for a new thing. No old things! They are passed away. Ha-ha.

"Markita, I was served divorce papers and I am scared. I don't want to sign them. We are leaders in the church. Some are telling me to hold on and others say move on. I don't know what to do."

My heart just sank a little for you because I know that feeling all too well. You want to fight for your marriage and believe God, then you go through all these emotions of should you sign on the dotted line or not. Take a deep breath, queen. You can't think about what others will perceive right now. This is about your life and what God is leading you to do. Do you really believe that God your father in heaven doesn't see what's going on? Sometimes the hardest thing to do in a situation like this is trust him even when it makes no sense to you. If your husband wants out of the marriage and you've done everything possible as a wife that you were supposed to do, from my heart to yours, let it go. Let go of what you may ask. Let go of proving to yourself how strong you must be. Let go of proving a point to people, even to yourself. If God allows it to be so, so it is. I know you love him. I know you want to keep your marriage together. But if his heart is hard and he is done, there is nothing you can do about his choice. Of course, you can pray, decree and declare, speak over him, anoint his clothes and shoes, write it down on a piece of paper "I'm not leaving!" (I've been there) but again he must change his mind about the marriage. Until he changes honey, you change. Change the way you're viewing this. You are not going to die. I promise you that you will heal. With the proper tools and help this will just be a testimony. I have no idea why you were served divorce papers, and it doesn't matter. You're not giving up on God if you sign the papers. The truth is God could be creating a way of escape for you. There could be a greater life in front of you and you keep holding on to this marriage. Being a leader in the church holds its own weight and pressure, you must live not just for the church but for you and if you have kids them too. Please don't stay in a marriage that is dead. If he wants out, release him. Love you.

"Markita, everyone in my family is divorced and I am still married, I feel like it's going to happen to me. I am scared."

Well let's not be scared! God has not given you a spirit of fear. Just because it happened to them, it doesn't mean it will happen to you. I am not saying to ignore the pattern in your family, but it can stop with you! Pray against divorce! Pray against separation! Pray for a joyful marriage. Pray God covers your marriage and no curse from the enemy can break your marriage up. Talk about how you feel to someone you trust with wisdom. Don't open yourself up to the lie that it will happen to you too. The devil is a liar! Cling to your husband and invite the holy spirit into your marriage. God is the head and he will lead you and your husband. Be the first in your family to have a healthy whole marriage. I am cheering you on!

"Markita, do you recommend counseling for me? I was just told to pray but I need more help than what I am getting."

I think that counseling is very healthy and good for everyone. We have been taught as Christians that we should just "pray about it". Yes, we should pray but sometimes therapy is what you need too. There are Christian counselors too. If you want to get counsel from a professional, I am down for that, but make sure they don't have you quote, read, and partake in things that a contrary to what God teaches us. I am so glad that you didn't allow the opinions of others to keep you from getting what you need.

"Markita, I rushed into my marriage and regret it. I love him, and he loves me but I really wasn't prepared."

Ok so here goes, you married someone, and you weren't prepared. What does that mean? Did you go through premarital counseling? If not, why not? Who married you? Did you get married for the wedding or for the covenant? You're an adult. You should have been honest before you got to this point. The question now is, are you willing to get the help you need? Love is a choice and marriage is work. It's not always perfect and pleasant. It comes with ups and downs. Give your marriage a fighting chance before giving up and reach out for help.

"Markita, do you still think about your exs'?"

Now why you wanna do me like that? Well this is "real raw and unkut!" It took years for me to really get them and especially my ex-husband out of me. I loved him. I thought we would be together forever and when that didn't happen it felt like I was dying inside. I was a part of him and he was a part of me. So, to say at times I don't think about him would be a lie. I then quickly remember why we are not together and thank GOD for my life with Shaun. See, I am not the woman that could still be his friend. It was all or nothing for me. I do wish him well, and I prayed (Because I don't keep praying for him) that he will love again and never do to a woman the things he did me. My last conversation with that man was the most freeing phone call in my life. He called me and asked me to forgive him and that he was so sorry for what he did to me. I told him these very words "I forgave you a long time ago. If I didn't I would never have been able to move on with my life. I release you in Jesus name. Please just don't ever put another woman through what you put me through. I prayed for your daughter too. That she will never experience pain from a man like her father. Protect her, cause one day she is going to be in love and you don't want her to come home crying to you about her prince charming broke her heart.

Never forget that I don't hate you, but I can never be your friend. Bless you."

I hung up the phone and cried my eyes out. Not because I was sad, but I knew then he couldn't play with my heart ever again. He may have had people in my family fooled but it was a done deal. I am an example that there's life after tragedy, injustice, shame, and disappointment. Yes, there's life and love on the other side of divorce.

14 *THE BOX*

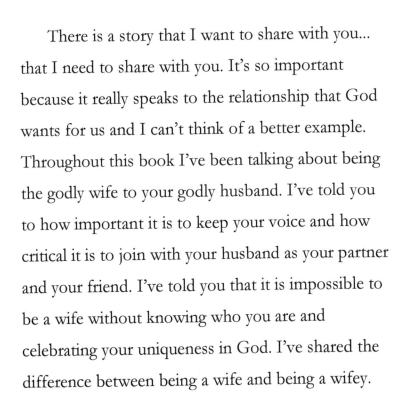

There is a story that I want to share with you... that I need to share with you. It's so important because it really speaks to the relationship that God wants for us and I can't think of a better example. Throughout this book I've been talking about being the godly wife to your godly husband. I've told you to how important it is to keep your voice and how critical it is to join with your husband as your partner and your friend. I've told you that it is impossible to be a wife without knowing who you are and celebrating your uniqueness in God. I've shared the difference between being a wife and being a wifey.

I've talked about not being a side-chick and not emasculating your man.

I've talked about the importance of repenting and renewing your mind. That is so necessary.

Now I want to talk about what is available to you in being his "good thang". What's the payoff? Why bother doing all this work? Why seek to have a godly husband in the first place?

A godly husband is your covering. Yes. He is the keeper of your heart. He is the buffer between you and everything else, including your past. He is your leader and you two are now knitted together by a godly bond. A godly husband is a natural representation of God in the family. He is to lead with compassion being trustworthy, consistent, available and accessible. He is to serve his family as a leader and he is to lead his family to righteousness. The godly husband is known as a Servant Leader. He is humble before God and strong through God in standing for his family. He seeks God for direction and stands on scripture as the revealed Truth. Listen to me! Even if he is not there. Yet it is your job to speak that over him. See him there, ok?

The reality is that no husband leads because he is worthy to lead. The truth is that no one is really sufficient to so great a task. There are at least a million ways we fall short. He knows it. He is aware of it every day. And yet a godly husband doesn't walk away or faint under the weight of it. He refocuses on what God requires of him. He trusts God and believes that whatever God has brought him to He has also prepared him to receive with great success. Where he feels weak and ill-prepared, he turns to God for guidance and assurance.

A godly husband is not intimidated by his wife's success and accomplishment. He knows that she is not only a reflection of the God who dwells within her, but she represents him as well. They are a partnership. Remember the virtuous woman in Proverbs 31? Remember how her husband regarded her? There was no competition between them. He respected and honored her. He even admired her.

While the husband is the leader and head of the family, he is secure enough in himself that he can support his wife in the use of her gifts, talents, skills and abilities without his masculinity being threatened. It is society that has created an unnecessary competition between the gender roles. "Wife" does not mean helpless, sitting at home, waiting for her man to arrive and take care of her. According to scripture, it sounds to me like they are doing well enough between them that there are servants in the home to help maintain it. It seems to me that both the godly wife and husband are skilled in delegation and time/resource management. Where neither of them relinquishes the intimate responsibilities of the home and family… only those where their energy and personal attention are not a necessity.

Your husband has stewardship over the family and ultimate responsibility before God for his family. In importance, he is to place you above himself and below God. I know you've heard it before, but scripture says that the husband is to love his wife... you... as Christ loves the church. What does that mean exactly? It means that he is to love you selflessly. He is to regard you as precious and valuable. He is to love you more than his own life. Your husband is to lead with the mind of Christ, always seeking God's wisdom and perfect will. He prays over and for you and is a good father to your children. You are to cover him in prayer and be his helpmeet, helpmate and peace.

Your husband works to be a good communicator for the sake of the relationship while you're a good listener and vice versa. He makes an effort to hear your heart and to understand without judgment. He seeks first to understand, then to be understood. He makes every attempt to hear with the heart of compassion with an intention to instigate peace. He also recognizes the challenge that it may be for him to express himself clearly. He acknowledges and surrenders to the communication process. And with your loving understanding and patience, his communication skills improve and so do yours.

In the same way that you spend time alone with God, so does your husband. He has a lot of responsibility towards his family and he seeks first God's kingdom and righteousness. He acknowledges God in all of his ways so that God will direct his paths and add success to his footsteps. He keeps God first above all else.

God's plan for your marriage is to create a union of souls that honor Him with their all. Your husband is the catalyst for all of that. He leads you in prayer as well as allows you to stand for him in his weakness. Because he loves and follows God so closely, he can be vulnerable with you as his partner and the lover of his soul.

Your husband is to be a visionary for your family.

There should be a core desire to move forward and upward. He should be the depository for new, witty, God-given ideas. He is not satisfied with mediocrity but seeks greater in God. He holds the vision for who your family is to be in the community and the kingdom.

Your husband is to be the protector of his family. Now let me be clear. I'm not talking about taking anybody down in the alley. He should not have to be an Ultimate Fighting Champion to have your respect and appreciation. Sure, it feels great to know your man can throw down, if need be. But protection also means something a bit more subtle.

Your husband sees too. He sees who's for you and who's not. He wants to be that shield for you. He doesn't want you to ever be without. He doesn't want anyone to hurt you and that is not him being obsessive, that's him being a MAN! For example, it could be late at night and I may want a drink or snack because I work late. I am a grown woman and can get up and go, but my husband would be offended. He wouldn't let me go anywhere. But because I want it, he would stop what he is doing and go for me, making sure I am home safe. Got that? See how that is an element of protection? Wouldn't you feel valued and highly regarded? This is who your husband is as a protector. There may also be times when he must stand for you to protect you from emotional and spiritual attack as well.

The amazing part is who your husband becomes to you. He is your love. He is your best friend. He is able to touch places in you that no one else on earth can. He is able to stand for you and protect you from the world.

He knows things about you and it doesn't scare him off. Your husband is willing to stand with you through it all.

This is who my husband became for me, and more. I could never have imagined the love we would have and the trust that would build between us. My past wasn't the greatest and I came with tons of pain, but Shaun loved me through it all. My husband isn't perfect, but he is perfect for me. We continue to grow in love and respect for each other, finding new depths of connection that just amaze and astound me. He is an amazing man and an amazing man of God... a man of wisdom. I watch him continue to grow in the Lord. He leads our family steadfastly and with certainty. He supports me in every way. He forgives me. He encourages me in my spirit and soul. He stands for my best and my success. He's confident in who I am and I can be authentically, unapologetically who God created me to be.

We've been through a lot together. From baby mama drama, family drama, money, kids, ministry and more. As a matter of fact I was seeing his cousin. Yes, I know... shocking! Let me tell you that I thought I was going to be connected to his cousin for the long haul, but the whole time he wasn't serious about me at all. He liked me and cared about me but wasn't trying to build. I was over it, so I just decided to do what I wanted to do. Shaun went to him and told how he really felt about me and his cousin told him basically to pursue me because I wasn't important to him like that. Well, I am glad

Shaun did! We are here to stay and not going nowhere! That's right, many tried it, but it was a no-go. My Shaun helped me be at peace with my past and all I had been through, I could share with him. No secrets. There was a turning point early on in our relationship that speaks to what it's like to be with a godly husband.

When you and I started this journey together, I shared with you my story. Remember in my story, I told you that I left Atlanta, Georgia after my ex and I got divorced. I was on the road when I found out the divorce was final. I drove all the way from Atlanta with a box of tissues, my gospel CD and just enough money to get me home. I also had "The Box." "The Box" has come to symbolize my journey. It represents all that I have been through. It represents the point of no return for me. "The Box" is my surrender to Shaun Collins as my husband and my choice. Here's another part of my story…

It was the day before my wedding to Shaun. I'll never forget, I was cleaning out my old closet at my mother and father's house. Deep in the back of the walk-in closet, this box was covered with clothes and shoes and other boxes. It had been there for years. You know the saying "Out of sight, out of mind", though somewhere in the back of my mind, just under the surface of consciousness, I knew it was there. And I knew it was good for me to go through some of the things in this closet because Shaun and I were moving into our apartment. As I took the items out of this larger box, I realized what that box was… and I paused… and I froze. It had been so long since I had seen that box. So long since I had thought of that box and all that it contained. I was pulled into times past. It scared me. All of the memories of what I went through and all of the things I remembered… that I had collected, were in that box and they all came flooding back to me. Everything was in there – postcards, letters, cards, memorabilia, pictures, money, jewelry, knickknacks, teddy bears, even lingerie – was all in that box. So I pulled the box out of the closet, lifted it up and was holding it tightly… almost hugging it. The box was very, very heavy.

I made it to the top of the stairs and I called for Shaun to come from the family room. He met me at the bottom of the stairs, looking up at me. I told him quietly that I needed to tell him something. He was silent waiting for me to continue. I was so scared. I said, "Shaun. This box. I've got to get rid of it." He asked me what was in the box and I told him it had "some things from my past." And I put my head down. He asked me what I was going to do with it. And I said, "I have to get rid of it because I can't marry you tomorrow knowing what's in this box." And I began to cry as I started down the stairs. At the same time, he started up the stairs and met me halfway. And again, the box was heavy, but I was holding it as if I could carry the weight by myself. As I neared him, Shaun extended his hands toward me as if to take the box from me. I was holding the box out but at the same time I didn't want to let the box go. I knew… I knew in my heart that when I let the box go I was completely letting go of all of my past. My past with my ex-husband, the past with all the things that I've gone through. As if he could sense my struggle, Shaun so gently and so sweetly, rubbed my hand and said, "It's okay, babe, it's okay. I'll get rid of it for you." What did he just say, I thought to myself? And the tears began to flow even harder from my eyes. And my heart began to race. Shaun took the box from my hands and he told me, "You'll never see this again." When I heard that, I thought, okay, we're gonna get rid of this box together. So of course, with good ole Kita strength, I'm following behind him and then he turned, looked back at me, and said, "I'm gonna get rid of the box." Then he walked out of the front door. I watched him carry that box to the car and pull off. I don't know to this day what he did with that box. I don't know if he burned it. I don't know if he threw it in the river. I don't know if he dumped it in the trash. All I know is that I saw my then-fiancé take something from me that was so heavy I could hardly bear the weight of it. After years of hiding under the shame of that box and all that it meant, he looked me in the eyes and told me I'd never see this box again and I didn't have to worry about it. I knew then that no matter what I was going to go through with Shaun or what we'd have to face, he was my husband. Some asked "Why did you tell Shaun?" "Couldn't you get anyone else to help you get rid of it?" and those are good questions. I even thought about just telling my father or mother, they would've handle it for me. But I had to be honest. He needed to see that just as much I needed to let it go. He needed to feel the weight of that box too. When I tell you this, Shaun made me feel so safe. He didn't make me feel like I was crazy or like something was wrong with me for holding on to something for so many years and still having the emotional attachments to it. He rescued me. Shaun instantly became my hero. I thought of what Jesus said in His Word, to cast your cares upon Me because I care for you. I'm a burden-bearer. I'm a

heavy load-sharer. I nailed your sins and sickness
and your burdens and all of that to the cross.
I watched my God-given husband walk away with all
of my shame, all of my grief, all of my sorrow, all of
my rejection, and all of my self-hatred in that box.
And I trusted him. And I loved him even more.
And I finally let it all go.

MARKITA D. COLLINS

15 RX FOR HEALING

I am so glad that you made it to this point. One thing nobody can say to me ever is that God is not a healer and that he is not concerned about our mental and physical wellbeing. God healed me emotionally from heartbreak and rejection, addiction, depression and physically from sickness and disease.

The following information is very powerful. I encourage you to try them. Here are the scriptures I read, the words I said, and the very practical things I did daily for MY healing. For me, I had to use my God given authority and get my life back! My prayer for you is that you're able to use these tools to help you get your life back too!

Every day, that's right every day until I felt a release, I forgave my exes, ex-husband, former friends, business partners, spiritual leaders and other people who offended and hurt me. Believe me when I say that it wasn't easy, but it was necessary. I could no longer be the victim! God showed me how victimization was a stronghold that was trying to prevent me from loving and trusting again. I wanted to love again, so being bitter and angry was not an option for me any longer. The devil wasn't going to steal my joy another day. I spoke the Word of God over myself.

For Emotional Healing, these are the things I said:

I forgive "_____" until I don't feel the urge or pull to make him/them feel what I endured. Help me God to release them out of my heart. Unknit every ungodly bond and demonic attachment. I choose to forgive for my freedom. Matthew 18:21-22 King James Version: "[21]Then came Peter to him, and said, Lord, how oft shall my brother sin against me, and I forgive him? Till seven times? [22]Jesus saith unto him, I say not unto thee, until seven times, but, until seventy times seven."

I release myself from all anger and fear. I release myself from all bitterness and revenge. God you have NOT given me a spirit of fear! You've given me Power, Love, and a sound mind! 2 Timothy 1:7: "For God hath not given us the spirit of fear, but of power, and of love, and of a sound mind." I am not weak; I am strong!

1.   I forgive myself. I will love again! I will use what I went through as lessons on what not to do or accept regarding relationships.

2.   My mind is transformed, I am changing the way I think about myself and how the world views me! Romans 12:2 "And be not conformed to this world, but be ye transformed by the renewing of your mind…" Proverbs 23:7 "For as he thinketh in his heart, so is he…..

3.   I am a whole woman. Not half, not a quarter, but a complete, whole woman. There is

nothing broken about me or within me. I will not experience this kind of loss again. God is restoring the years now. Joel 2:25: "And I will restore to you the years that the locusts hath eaten, the cankerworm, and the caterpillar, and the palmerworm, my great army which I sent among you."

4.   I will love again with no limits and let people love me unconditionally. I refuse to be in the way of the blessings God is sending me.

For Emotional Healing, these are the things I did:

I.   I mentioned it before and I am saying it again!! Why? Faith comes by hearing. So, hear this again just in case you bypassed it...Forgive! Forgiveness is key to your healing. If you hold on to offense and not forgive, bitterness will grow, and spiritual corrosion can occur. So, you must forgive people and do it quickly.

Remember Jesus teaches us to forgive seventy times (Matthew 18:21-22). Look at it this way. You freely walked yourself into a prison cell and lock the door. Check this out, you have the key to unlock it and get out but refuse to use your key. Don't lock yourself in a personal prison.

II.   This works! Have an erase ceremony (old and new texts, emails, social media contacts, direct messages, pictures, voicemails and videos etc.) – **Block:** No more access, no more interference. **Delete:** Get it out your face. You don't need to be reminded of the thing that hurt, until you're healed and overcome the pain.

   Trash: Go a step above delete! Get rid of it for good. With delete you can still recover the info, but when you "trash" it, it's gone for good!

III. Be around positive people. Intentionally have fun and laugh. Laughter is like medicine. According to Proverbs 17:22, "A merry heart doeth good [like] a medicine, but a broken spirit drieth the bones." Do not entertain negative people and their opinions.

IV. Pray and worship daily; fast and consecrate by turning away my plate, turning off the phone, the television, and social media. Make time for God and come away from the noise and chatter for a while.

V. Be honest with yourself and with the . He already knows how you really feel. Do not pretend to be ok and you're not.

VI. Do not be against therapy. Sometimes you need to sit and talk it out with a certified, trained professional during your healing process.

VII. Read the Bible and books that revive and refresh the spirit. Listen to powerful worship and praise music.

God also healed my body and delivered me from Graves' disease. I had been challenged with that for nearly ten years. There are times when the symptoms try to manifest but I believe the report of the Lord! I am healed! I even decided to get weight loss surgery because I made up my mind that I deserve to live my best life. Having the procedure done wasn't me saying I don't trust God, no I had to trust him even the more. He broke addiction to food off my life! I am not ashamed to say it. Yes, He can do the same for you.

For Physical Healing, these are the things I said:

1)   Healing belongs to me! Not sickness and disease. Deuteronomy 7:15: "And the LORD will take away from thee all sickness and will put none of the evil diseases of Egypt, which thou knowest, upon thee, but will lay them upon all that hate thee."

2)   I am healed by the Word of God. Isaiah 53:5: "But he was wounded for our transgressions, he was bruised for our iniquities: the chastisement of our peace was upon him; and with his stripes we are healed."

3)   My body is the temple of the HOLY GHOST. I know what the facts say but they are not the truth. The truth is I am healed in Jesus' name! I break cycles and generational curses of sickness off my life. I confess with my mouth that my faith has risen today. Hebrews 11:1: "Now faith is the substance of things hoped for, the evidence of things not seen."

4)   No weapon formed against my body or emotions shall be able to prosper! Isaiah 54:17: "No weapon that is formed against thee shall prosper;

and every tongue that shall rise against thee in judgment thou shalt condemn. This is the heritage of the servants of the LORD, and their righteousness is of me, saith the LORD."

5)   I will trust the Lord even in sickness! He wants me to be well. 3 John 1:2: "Beloved, I wish above all things that thou mayest prosper and be in health, even as thy soul prospereth."

For Physical Healing, these are the things I did:

1)   I took the medication prescribed! I prayed over it and took it until I felt a release not to take it anymore.

2)   I obeyed God and fasted for 22 days. I did a dry fast, a water fast, and then a fruit and veggie regimen. Whatever God said, I did. I was desperate and determined to be healed. Also, I fast for health reasons and spiritual. Always fast as led.

3)   My journey was different from other people. I prayed and asked GOD for the release to

have an operation called the VSG Vertical sleeve gastrectomy.

4)   I still walk and exercise at least 4 times a week.

5)   I spend time making me better.

6)   I read the Bible and speak the scripture over and over. Remember faith come by hearing.

7)   I recommend that if you need to take medication for mental disease, please do not be ashamed of that, and ask the Lord to help you with the process. You are not weird, crazy or strange. It's ok, until you are delivered, and God makes you whole in your mind take your Rx. Please don't allow pride to keep you bound. You look free on the outside but in chains on the inside.

8)   This is not a one-time thing. Wash, rinse and repeat until change comes!

ABOUT THE AUTHOR

Gleaming with an abundant amount of gratitude, delivering heart-felt messages with passion, and walking with unshakable conviction, Markita D. Collins is living proof that spirit-driven purpose generates boundless blessings and undeniable success.

CEO Markita D. Collins is a bestselling author, top 100 international live streaming social media influencer who is helping to shape the minds of many, as an entrepreneur, prophetess, minister, recording artist, anointed mentor, certified life coach and advisor. Her rapidly growing empire includes The Unbreakable Experience, VIP power sessions, Unbreakable Retreats, GIRL TALK with KITA, Kita's Kookies and Treats, Kita's Kompany and Imagine Media, LLC. Collins resides in Pennsylvania with her husband Shaun, their two boys and twin girls.

For booking information regarding speaking and ministering at special events, private consulting or media interviews, please contact Team Markita D. Collins at: staff@MarkitaDCollins.com. To learn about classes, coaching and other Markita D. Collins resources, visit MarkitaDCollins.com.

I'M STILL OLD FASHIONED!

NOTES

NOTES

I'M STILL OLD FASHIONED!

NOTES

NOTES